FOOTBALL BOOTS AND NO CONDOMS

John Hayes

FOOTBALL BOOTS AND NO CONDOMS

John Hayes

ISBN 9781914615108

A CIP catalogue record for this book
is available from the British Library

Published 2021 Tricorn Books
Aspex Portsmouth
42 The Vulcan Building
Gunwharf Quays
Portsmouth PO1 3BF
Printed & bound in the UK

FOOTBALL BOOTS AND NO CONDOMS

Contents

Chukka boots

Portsdown Modern Secondary School For Young Gentlemen was the sign on the entrance gates. Where the young gentlemen came from was a question that Johnny could never work out, as he never knew any young toffs at Portsdown.

The school uniform was only worn by the few privileged boys. Most of the other boys' school uniform was a donkey jacket, jeans and Chukka boots. A donkey jacket was a three-quarter length, heavy-clothed coat with imitation leather shoulder pads, jeans were ice blue, or Wranglers, and Chukka boots were black suede boots with a crepe soul, some an inch thick, jeans were with three-inch turn-ups, most as tight to the skin as possible (care of Mrs Callard, the local seamstress).

"Sit down," came the order from the Form 3A master, a rather well-built gent, clothed in teacher clothes, well-pressed trousers held up with a large leather buckled belt, blue shirt (starch-collared), blazer with a RAF badge on the breast pocket, a striped tie loose at the neck. A red flushed freshly shaven face with thin lips and a large forehead, all covered with a head of red thick tufted hair.

"Welcome to Class 3A. My name is Mr Evans. I run a tight ship, so if you behave you'll find it a pleasure to be in my form, if you step out of line, the consequences will be like nothing you have experienced, do you understand?"

He waited for an answer but none was forthcoming. The boys of 3A just looked down to the ground or casually out of the nearest window, they had heard it all before, every year, every class the same old threats.

"Any questions?"

With that a hand shot up into the air.

"Sir!" It was Barry Houghton.

"Yes, what's your name, boy?"

"Houghton, sir."

"Well what's your question, Houghton?"

"Sir, by the look of your badge you were in the airforce."

"Yes," came the reply from a puzzled teacher.

"Well sir, how can you run a tight ship if you were in the RAF?"

The class tried not to giggle, knowing what was next.

"We have a comedian in the class. Mr Houghton, will you please join me at my desk?"

Barry pushed his chair back, deliberately scraping it on the stone floor, the noise vibrating around the silent classroom. This caused a small outbreak of the giggles.

"I take note of your comments, Houghton, and as this is our first encounter, if you apologise for making your last remark you can return to your desk." The ball was in Barry's court.

"Well boy? What's your answer?"

"Sir, I thought it was a good question."

With that, Mr Evans shook his head.

"If you thought being cheeky was a good question…"

"I did sir, and I don't think I was being cheeky, just inquisitive."

Johnny whispered to Micky, "He must have swallowed a dictionary to come out with 'inquisitive'."

Micky laughed but out loud.

"Laughing? Who else thinks it's funny?" Mr Evans surveyed the class. Johnny and Micky kept their heads lowered, but they couldn't stop giggling.

"Well, Mr Houghton, it seems you have a few fans who think it's funny to undermine my authority." Mr Evans remained calm, as he went to the long cupboard standing in the corner. The class knew what was going to be extracted from the tall brown cupboard. Why was it concealed? Every other teacher had it on full display on the desk in front of them and every class knew it was hanging over them like it's the Sword of Damocles.

"Sir, why is it wrong to question you on your wording?" Barry had a point, after all we were 3A, the cream of 'Portsdown Academy For Young Gentlemen'. The class hummed in agreement.

"Houghton." Mr Evans was lost for words; he didn't know the class he had inherited.

Barry stood his ground, as the cane inflicted its will on his long goalkeeping fingers.

Two strokes were admonished, one on each hand.

"Well Houghton," Mr Evans said, adding, "An apology please."

Barry never budged.

"Houghton, an apology."

Barry never budged.

"Houghton!" Mr Evans was getting mad, his patience was growing thinner and thinner.

Barry kept his hands held out, his face as determined as ever not to give in.

Mr Evans laughed. "Put your hands down, Houghton! OK 3A, you have a mind of your own but it's up to you if you want to learn or ruin your futures."

The boys of 3A knew they had a teacher who would stand by them and tolerate a few misdemeanour's on their way to an education.

So life in 3A had begun with a bang.

"OK," Mr Evans said, "can we please do the register."

The class answered to their names in alphabetical order,

Upsall being the last name called.

"Upsall," Mr Evans repeated his name twice. "I believe you have a tendency to be late for school."

"I know sir, but it's not my fault it's my pigeons," Upsall answered.

"Well you know the rules. Late three times and it's the slipper."

It was then the class noticed a large well-worn slipper hanging on a hook at the front of Mr Evans' desk. So that's what replaced the cane, Hazer thought.

Latecomers

The first few weeks went by quietly, until Terry Upsall, who had been late once or twice, decided to hit the treble.

The school gates were shut promptly at 8.55 am so pupils could be in class for registration at 9 am before going to assembly for prayers, hymns, and a morning lecture from the head Mr Digby.

On the gate each morning was the duty master ready to close the gate at exactly 8.55 am. Some teachers were a bit more lenient and allowed the occasional latecomer one or two minutes after the bell had sounded.

But it was Mr Evans' week on duty at the gate. He was old school, as stated before, an ex-RAF bomber crew member, never was a tutor more punctual than Mr Evans!

The rule was, late three times in one week and Mr Size 10 Slipper was visiting your backside on six occasions.

It was Friday 8.50 am. Terry had been late on Monday and Wednesday in that week.

Monday: the boys stood at their desks as Mr Evans entered, followed by Terry who looked like he had just run the four-minute mile faster than Roger Bannister.

"Sit," came the order from Mr Evans.

"Upsall."

"Yes sir," came Terry's staunch reply.

The class were all ears, awaiting Terry's excuse for being late.

"Why are you late? And on my watch?" Mr Evans boomed.

Terry looked puzzled, then endeavoured to make an excuse he hadn't used on a previous occasion. "Sir, are you sure your watch is correct, because I left home in plenty of time."

"My watch is correct. Perhaps it was your watch which was slow, Mr Upsall," Mr Evans enquired.

"That's not possible," Terry replied.

"And why not, Upsall?"

"I ain't got a watch," Upsall chirped, turning to the class like a comedian delivering the punchline.

The class could see it coming, as Mr Evans fell for it hook, line and sinker.

Simmons and Faithfull burst out laughing, followed by the rest of 3A.

"OK Upsall, now tell me why you were late." Mr Evans' patience was starting to run out.

"Well sir – and this is the honest truth on my dying death bed sir," Upsall said, while holding his hand on his heart, the other behind his back with his fingers crossed for all the class to see. "Well I left home at twenty to nine and it's only a ten-minute stroll from my front door to this wonderful institute of learning, sir." Upsall emphasised 'sir'.

"Cut the crap, Upsall!" Mr Evans was taking no prisoners.

"Well sir, honest sir, my next door but one, a lovely old lady at number 32, who by the way is a widow, lost her hubby in the war. RAF, I think sir, bomber command. Well sir, she was standing outside our house on the green under the tree, it's a lovely tree sir, lots of red berries in the winter (helps feed the birds when they're hungry, and in the spring it's full of the most colourful flowers, the birds love to sit in the branches singing to their hearts' content), but that's the trouble, sir. Mrs James' cat loves birds! To eat that is! Well, the silly old moggie got stuck up the tree. So there I was sir, in somewhat of a quandary. I could climb the tree and rescue Mrs James' cat and be late for school, or be on time for school and leave Mrs James, a widowed, disabled, old age pensioner, in tears. So I chose to rescue the moggie and bring a smile to Mrs James' weary old face and be late for school."

The class burst into a loud cheer. Terry turned to Hazer, Austin, Simmo and the rest of 3A and bowed as if he had just completed a Shakespeare sonnet at the Old Vic.

"Upsall, you were late." Then he added, "It goes in the book." Mr Evans was not for turning. In other words, he thought it was a load of bullshit, as did the rest of Upsall's class, but it was entertaining.

Tuesday: the class answered roll call all on time.

Wednesday morning arrived. It was 8.50 am. The gang, Hazer, Raff, Austin, Simmo, Faithfull and several other members of 3A were milling around by the school gate, Upsall was nowhere to be seen, Mr Evans took several glances at his watch, then in the distance some 400 yards away a young lad could be observed running for all his worth to make the gate before the bell sounded. Mr Evans could see Upsall sprinting, waving his arms now and again in earnest.

The lads pleaded with Mr Evans to let him reach his goal, but the pleas fell on deaf ears.

"Rules are rules," Mr Evans stated. "And I never made the rules," he added.

The bell sang out. Upsall was just 50 yards from his target but CLANG! The gate closed.

Upsall reached the gate, his face reddened from his efforts. His fingers clutched the wire mesh of the gate, his head bowed trying to catch his breath. He must have broken the school record for the 400 metres or, in those days, 440 yards. Boy, could he run!

The class waited behind their old Victorian desks, each boy stood to attention as Mr Evans entered, followed by Terry who looked absolutely shattered, his cheeks a rosy red, sinews of sweat dripping off his brow onto his nose, then dropping down to meet his large blueish lips. He licked the sweat with his tongue, still unable to talk, while he took deep breaths to fill his empty lungs.

"Upsall, why are you late again?" Mr Evans inquired. He had the look of a teacher within a teacher on his countenance. The class waited in anticipation.

"Well sir, this is the honest truth."

Mr Evans looked up to the ceiling, folding his arms, giving a small shake of his unruly head of hair.

"No stories or you'll end up like Pinocchio, Upsall." Mr Evans had cracked a joke. This was unheard of in all the history of Portsdown Secondary School For Young Gentlemen.

"It's all true, sir, honest!" Terry emphasised 'honest' again.

"Carry on," Mr Evans said as he ushered Terry to the front of the class, so each pupil could see his nose increasing in size with every whopper he came out with.

"Well sir, I keep pigeons and as you might know they are very unpredictable." Terry opened his excuse cautiously.

"Carry on," Mr Evans interrupted.

"I will sir, if you don't interrupt!" Terry replied.

Mr Evans smiled, awaiting the next fairy tale from Terry's lips.

"As you may know, sir, they are lovely birds and throughout history they have been used to carry messages by everyone, from the Romans to the present-day army. They have distinguished pigeon kind throughout history and time immemorial, saving many British lives. Well sir, Jack, he's my prize bird. Wouldn't come in the loft. Something or someone was upsetting him, I don't know what it could be, until I looked up into the branches of the tree that hangs over our garden, and there it was. Mrs James' moggie, and he was after my birds. As if he ain't got enough sparrows or starlings to eat, he's after my Jack! So I tried with all my heart to get him to come down, so I would be able to get Jack into the loft, but the moggie wouldn't budge, so after 15 minutes or so of trying to coax him down, I lost my rag, went indoors, got my caddy [catapult], put a large marble in the pouch and sorted Mrs James' cat out! In the process, the marble ricocheted off the moggie's backside and went through next door's greenhouse. Well, Mr Humphreys is a lovely neighbour, so I had to own up to my crime which took another ten minutes as he was still in bed, being another old age pensioner, so by the time I confessed and promised to pay for a new pane of glass, the clock was ten to nine, and you know the rest, sir!"

Upsall turned to the class for his applause which followed without exception.

"You're in the book, Upsall." Mr Evans was not convinced by Terry's fabricated tale, but Terry's nose never grew any longer so maybe he was telling the truth.

Thursday: no latecomers.

Friday: as usual, the gang were waiting at the school gates. Terry was nowhere in sight. As the clock hit 8.55 am, Mr Evans was pacing up and down like a sentry at Buckingham Palace, awaiting his nemesis' arrival or non-arrival. Soon the rest of 3A and half of the third-year boys were waiting at the gate, each trying to look above the head of the boy in front, everyone looking up Whitstable Road.

The bell rang. No sign of Upsall. The crowd had gathered for nothing, so the boys shambled back into school, muttering as they went.

Hazer hadn't given up. He kept looking back along Whitstable Road. Then he appeared, running like the wind, his arms flaying from side to side. A faint voice could be heard – "Hold the gate!" As the figure got nearer, the "Hold the gate!" grew louder and louder.

Mr Evans spun round as Terry's outstretched fingers clawed at the wired gate, a bit like a POW trying to escape from a stalag in Germany. Only he wanted to break in!

Mr Evans unlocked the gate to let Upsall into the hallowed walls of Portsdown Academy For Young Gentlemen. Terry's blond hair was all over his face, his shirt was buttoned up in the wrong sequence and his red braces (that was the style of the day) were only held onto his Wrangler jeans by one button at the back. He looked a mess and Mr Evans was quick to tell him so in no uncertain terms.

The class stood to attention as Mr Evans entered the room, followed by a dishevelled Upsall who was trying to recover his decorum in front of his eagerly waiting audience. He spent the next few minutes buttoning up his shirt in the correct sequence, tucking his shirt back in his ice blue jeans.

Mr Evans bade the class to sit, a clatter of chairs was his answer; the noise seemed to vibrate around the classroom.

"Well Upsall, what's your excuse for being late again?" Mr Evans was enjoying every moment, anticipating Terry's demise, as his own thoughts went back to his youth and his time in bomber command, and the day that if he wasn't late because of a puncture in the lorry taking him to his base, he would not be here teaching this mostly load of just-off-the-street boys. His thoughts seemed to mellow; his memories of his aircrew would never leave his side.

"You alright, sir?" Upsall said, expecting a terse response.

Mr Evans nodded, looked at the class, then turned to the blackboard to regain his composure, a tear came from nowhere and dribbled down his left cheek.

Terry was standing awaiting the executioner, his face still held a perpetual smile.

"Before I hear any more stories, Upsall, can you please tell the truth." Mr Evans definitely had a soft spot for Terry. It took Terry a while to answer. He was trying to remember his previous excuses. Well, that's what Hazer and his classmates were assuming.

"Well sir, you'll never believe me but this is the honest truth on my best mate's grave." Micky looked at Hazer, he looked at Micky, he looked at Davies, he looked at Simmo, he looked at Faithfull, he looked at Houghton, he looked at… so and so. So the whole class looked at each other because Upsall was a friend of everybody in 3A. Each one thinking, tell the truth or we're going to meet a grisly end!

Hazer had a smile above his nearly growing haired chin, Upsall winked. Hazer and Micky knew Terry had a belter!

"Well sir, you'll never believe this but it's true. Cross my heart, hope to die!"

With that, Terry crossed his heart.

"Carry on, Upsall." Mr Evans was getting impatient.

"It started when I woke up," Terry stated.

"I know," Mr Evans interrupted.

Then Mr Evans' thoughts went back to Tuesday.

"Sorry to interrupt your story, Upsall." The word 'story' was emphasised by Mr Evans.

"Sir, you'll never believe what happened," Upsall began.

"I know," Mr Evans interrupted again. He couldn't help himself.

"As I said sir, it's hard to believe but it's as true as I stand here in front of you and your illustrious pupils. As you may remember sir, it was absolutely piss…" He hesitated, stopping in mid-sentence. "…pouring down last night and I got drowned on the way home and because we are not very well off, I got this hole in my boots [Chukka boots, crepe soles, suede uppers] and I'm not due another pair till after Christmas holidays, so my socks were soaking wet through and I only got one pair cause my big brother Bobby nicked my other pair [socks were brightly coloured, shocking blue or pink were the style of the day, not school grey, they were for squares!].

"So my socks and the rest of my clothes were wringing wet, so my mum hung them up on the line that hangs up in our kitchen so they would be dry and ready for school this morning." Terry had a short break, his mind preparing for his next sentence. Mr Evans sat down behind his desk, his head moving from side to side.

"Well sir, I got up as usual, Mum brings me a cuppa Charlie at 7:45, so I bounced out of bed ready for another glorious day at this wonderful school. I went downstairs, it was 8 o'clock, and went out to my loft, let my pigeons out for a quick circuit, got them resettled in the loft, gave them their corn, then returned to the kitchen to put my clobber on. I takes me jimjams off, goes to put me Wranglers on but they were still a bit damp so Mum lit the oven [no tumble dryers in those days] and hung my jeans over the door. It was now 8:35 am. I said to Mum I'll be late for school if I don't hurry up, and she said you'll catch your death if you put wet clothes on, so the time was 8:40 am when she handed me my jeans, after putting them to her cheeks to make sure they were dried.

"I was ready in a jiffy. I was about to put my socks on when out of nowhere Mrs James's moggie flew out of the scullery, grabbed one of me socks and hightailed it out of the back door, which I had foolishly left open. My mum's always telling me off for not closing doors after me. How I diverse!"

Terry took another long pause.

"I was up like a rocket and chased him round our backyard, making the occasional dive to try and apprehend the moggie with the long pink tongue (my sock) hanging out of its mouth, but it was all to no avail. As I was barefooted, I stubbed my toe on the coal bunker step. And it didn't half hurt." He pointed to his injured foot. "I tried but in the end Mrs James' moggie had got his revenge for my catapult shot to his backside the other morning, so here I am. At your mercy, sir."

Mr Evans gave a slow handclap, saying, "Vivid imagination, Upsall," repeating "vivid, vivid" as the class gave a cheer. Mr Slipper was brought from its hook, placed on the desk in full view of the class.

"Upsall, rules are rules. Bend over," Mr Evans ordered.

As Terry bent over, his jeans rode up his legs. The class peered down at Terry's ankles. On one was a shocking pink sock, on the other just bare skin.

"Ouch that hurts."

"It's meant to, Upsall," Mr Evans replied.

Friday and Elvis

It was Friday. The weekend was upon the teenage boys' minds.

"What we doing tonight?" Hazer asked Austin.

"Don't know, what you reckon?" Micky turned to Upsall whose bum hadn't quite recovered from the six whacks it received from the size 11 enforcer.

"You could sleepover ours?" Micky Austin asked.

"Nah." Hazer shrugged, remembering the long walk to Bert's cafe.

"Can't anyhow, got a game tomorrow," Hazer added.

Raff had joined the gang at the school gates.

"Alright, how's your jacksie?" He inquired of Terry, a smile on his face.

"Still bleeding, killing me."

"What we doing tonight?" Raff asked.

"You could come over my home. I can borrow our Annette's record player," Terry suggested.

The boys were hoping Terry would support this option, for their hormones were starting to jump all over the place. It was Annette!

"Alright, see you later." The boys made their way home for tea, agreeing to meet round Micky's then strolling down to Terry's.

A couple of weeks before, the three visitors were in Terry's kitchen, when Annette walked in with just her bra covering her boobs. The boys nearly fainted. She reached up to the line, running across the kitchen ceiling to retrieve her top. Johnny's eyes nearly exploded. The two Mickys stood with their mouths wide open.

Annette never seemed to notice her three admirers as she clutched her blouse and left the kitchen. The boys were in shock, turning to each other. It was like they had been bewitched. No one spoke then Terry came into the kitchen.

"You lot alright?" He asked with a puzzled look on his face.

Johnny puffed his cheeks before replying, "Yeah, yeah." He could feel a rather uncomfortable lump in his jeans. Annette had that way with men and boys but, he was just a 13-year-old. Micky and Micky remained silent as they followed Terry up to his room to listen to Elvis the pelvis on Annette's Dansette record player.

That's why it was a good idea to go to Terry's on a Friday night not Bert's cafe.

The boys arrived at Terry's. He ushered them into the hallway. Mrs Upsall and Mr Upsall were ready for the pub. It was Friday and they always used the Clacton on Fridays.

"You boys help yourself to the lemonade in the kitchen."

"Thanks Mrs Upsall," Raff answered, the others nodded. Plummy had joined Hazer and Raff at the shop before they met Micky A. Plummy was a year older than Hazer, but had become a good mate to the gang since moving to Wymering from Portsea in the Easter holidays.

"I'll get the lemonade," Raff offered.

"No I'll get it," Hazer said. The only reason was the chance to see Terry's older sister and maybe another glimpse of her in her bra.

"I'll get it later," Terry said as he beckoned the boys up the stairs. As they ascended the stairs, a bedroom door opened. Raff's eyes grew the size of sauces, Hazer, Micky A and Plummy gulped as Annette stood at the top of the stairs.

"You boys better not scratch my records," she said.

"We wha... wha... won't," Plummy uttered as she brushed past the boys on the stairs. The silence was embarrassing.

As she passed each boy, they couldn't stop their goggle eyes looking at her breasts.

Terry stood at the bottom of the stairs, a smile on his rosy cheeks. He knew what his mates were thinking.

So the records played, mostly Elvis. Lemonade was drunk. Time to go home and bed, ready for footy in the morning.

As Johnny lay in his bed, he recalled the day Plummy came into the gang.

The gang were playing football on the green in front of Johnny's house when this strange looking boy stopped to watch. The stranger was dressed in a jean jacket (very rare and expensive), tight blue jeans, coloured socks and winklepickers (these were the most trendy shoes of the day, no one could afford winklepickers unless they were working).

His face was that of a shrew – pointed nose, his chin was spotted with a few teenage spots, his ears were like an elf's, his hair was thin and straggly, as was his body. A strange-looking boy indeed, Johnny had thought at the time.

The ball went into the road and was about to roll down the hill, when strange-looking boy chased it, picked it up and carried it back to the pitch.

"Cheers, mush!" Raff said.

"That's alright," strange boy replied.

"Wanna play? We're one man down on our side," Erky inquired.

"I ain't very good."

Strange boy was true to his word. He was hopeless but he kept moving, making everyone laugh with his attempts at footy. Falling over, missing the ball completely when trying to kick it. He had the gang in stitches. Especially when they put him in goal and the ball hit him, smacking his face.

After the game, the inquest started on where he came from, what school he was from.

"What's your name?" Rolfie asked.

"Dave," came the reply.

"Dave what?" Raff interrupted.

Plummy replied, "Peach."

Micky A. said, "Don't like peaches, love plums."

So his nickname was born. 'Plummy' joined the Peterborough Road gang. He was still wearing the same clothes 19 months later with his winklepickers curled up like Aladdin's slippers.

Johnny got home about 10 o'clock, and Jock was still on the beer. Johnny's mum was sitting by the TV set (black and white 12" screen) watching the *Black and White Minstrel Show*. His sisters Jeannie, Linda and Mo sitting on the floor, Debbie in her pram, being gently rocked by Jeannie, the open fire was dying in the grate.

"Had a good night?" Johnny's mum asked.

"Yeah, went down Terry's listening to Elvis on his record player." Johnny lied about it being Terry's record player as he had been pestering his mum for one for Christmas.

"Night mum. I got footy in the morning."

The caped cheat

Johnny was up at 8 o'clock, had a quick wash, pulled his footy kit off the clothesline in the front room, which was now strewn with empty bottles of beer (Jock had had a carry out – a carry out was when you brought home booze after the pubs had closed and carried on drinking indoors). The house stunk of stale booze. He quickly put on his footy kit, then he pulled on his young man's tracksuit which was two sizes too big. Bought for his birthday, this was the smallest size available so he had to fold the waist over a couple of times. The top was okay. He pulled his bumper boots on, tying the laces in a double bow. Bumper boots were like plimsolls only with high ankles with two bullseye-like plastic moulds to signify the make on the sides.

Johnny met Raff and they both strolled down to the Cosham bus terminal which was positioned next to the railway station. The terminal was a Victorian constructed, cast-iron building about 40 foot long, and 12 feet wide. Its facade was quite ornate, with the roof shaped like a Chinese pagoda. It was painted in red and cream (the colour of Portsmouth bus company), and was lined with slatted bench seats around the inside walls with the rafters showing on the inside. The boys would swing from these a bit like monkeys, often imitating their long-lost Darwinian cousins.

When they arrived, most of the rest of the team were waiting.

"Alright mush," Jacko greeted Hazer with a smile on his face. Jacko was the captain, the rest of the lads were too busy watching Upsall doing his impressions of a Barbary ape swinging from one rafter to another.

"Morning boys," a stern voice echoed through the building followed by, "Get down Upsall." Terry dropped to the ground.

"Morning sir," the football team replied in unison.

Mr Wally Wharton, a 6-foot, well-built man, in his early 40s, he was clean shaven with a square-jowled chin and thick dark eyebrows which were topped with Brylcreem-parted brown hair.

Mr Wally Wharton was the 3rd and 4th year football team manager. He taught the C and D class boys so most of the team who were A and B class boys never encountered him in class, but according to Plummy and Micky Copus who were in his class, he could inflict pain unheard of with the bamboo silencer.

"OK, gather round, I've got your bus tickets [issued by the school for away games]." The boys held their hands out to receive the small cinema-like tickets, one for going one for the return journey.

The bus arrived according to the timetable. It was ten minutes late, the destination 'Southsea Common' was emblazoned on the front above the driver's cockpit. Underneath were other significant stops – Twyford Avenue, North End, Lake Road, Guildhall – then the last stop, Southsea. The boys shuffled on the bus, to a man climbing up the stairs to get the best seats (window seats, these were the prize ones, being at the front of the bus).

All the team managed to get seated when the bus conductor pressed the bell signalling the driver to move off.

"Fares please," the conductor would call out as he doled out the tickets from the rounded, metal ticket holder. He turned the handle as if cranking a car (most cars in Johnny's early years had handles to start them if the batteries went flat).

The boys were doing the usual boy stuff, throwing rolled

up bits of paper, wetting their fingers and putting it in the lughole of the unsuspecting boy in front of them, who gave out a "Fuck off, you wanker" to his assailant.

As the bus neared its destination, Mr Wharton, who had been sitting in the lower deck of the bus, ascended the steps. Just as the footy boot flew past and hit the back window. It fell at his feet.

"Whose foot does this belong to?" He inquired.

"Mine, sir," Faithfull said, expecting to get a whack.

But Wally was in a good mood. He picked it up and handed it to Terry F.

"You can't play with one boot," he laughed, adding, "in fact, you have a job to play with two." He laughed out loud, expecting the team to join in with his humour, but they were too busy talking amongst themselves.

"Was that a joke, sir." Faithfull was quite offended.

"Yes Faithfull, it was a joke." Wally shook his head.

The team disgorged from the double decker bus. The Southsea Common football pitches were the worst in Portsmouth by a country mile.

On this Saturday, the wind was blowing in from the Solent at 30 miles an hour. The rain drifted across the pitches, filling the puddles in each goalmouth.

"We can't play in that," Mr Wharton was telling the opposition team's schoolmaster.

"We can't call it off," the other master insisted, adding, "it's only a shower."

Mr Wharton turned to the boys. "It's up to you but if we don't play they are going to claim the points." Under the rules, the team deemed not to have turned up would lose the points to the opposition. This was what the other schoolmaster was hoping would happen. The team looked at each other. "We'll give it a go, sir," Jacko said. The boys grunted in agreement.

So into the green council shed they filed. The other team were already halfway to getting their clothes back on, thinking the game was off.

"Bloody hell! He's fucking mad!" came a voice from the other team.

So with great reluctance, 22 young footy-mad boys took to the pitch with the wind and rain beating into their forlorn looking faces.

As was custom, the home team's master was called upon to referee the game so it was that 'he's fucking mad' dressed in waterproof trousers, socks tucked into them, a waterproof cape, a sou'wester hat (as you see fishermen wear) bounded out of his changing room holding the leather 'T' ball under one arm and whistle and linesman flags under the other.

The boys lined up and the coin was tossed into the air by the home team's captain. "Tails" was called by Jacko, the coin went into the mud. The ref (he who's fucking mad) bent down to retrieve the coin, couldn't find it in the mud so lied, "It's heads!"

"We'll stay as we are," he added. "I'm supposed to say that," the opposing skipper said.

"Get on with it, boy," came his terse reply.

So the game kicked off. The ball could hardly move in the puddles, most of the boys were too cold to bother chasing after the ball, a few had their hands inside their shirts to keep them warm. The caped crusader kept encouraging his team, then with the ball five yards outside of the Portsdown penalty box, one of his players fell over in the mud. No Portsdown player was near him. In fact, Kimber the full back was too busy trying to keep warm – an elephant could have gone through the gap without being tackled by him.

The whistle blew. Both teams stopped wondering what was wrong. The crusader pointed to the penalty spot.

"What? No way!" came a shout from a Portsdown defender. "I wasn't anywhere near him, he fell over in the mud."

The player had spilled the ball, tripped over his standing leg and slid in the mud. Even so, he was still a yard outside the penalty box.

"He ain't even in the box!" came another outburst from the defender. The ref picked up the ball and preceded to the penalty spot.

"Don't argue with me or you'll be off."

Someone behind him shouted, "You cheating wanker."

He turned round. "Who said that?"

Nobody said a word. Johnny looked over to Mr Wharton but he was nowhere in sight. He had retired after the rain to have a fag in the dressing rooms, leaving the linesman's fluttering flag stuck in the mud awaiting his return.

So the penalty was given (in those days, most public pitches never had nets for the goals).

A large lad took the kick. It flew to Houghton's right. He had outguessed the kicker, his right fists punched the ball clear.

"Well done!" A cheer went up.

The crusader blew his whistle again and pointed to the spot. "He moved," he shouted (the goalie must not move till the ball is kicked).

"Fucking wanker," came from the Portsdown boys.

"I fu…fu…king didn't move!" Houghton was furious.

"You did. Take it again," came the order from the caped assassin.

The same boy took the kick. He took a ten-yard run-up and blasted the ball over the bar.

The whistle rang out. Both teams prepared themselves for a goal kick but Mr He's Fucking Mad grabbed the ball and pointed to the halfway line indicating it was a goal. Both teams had seen the ball clear the crossbar by at least ten feet but as there were no nets it was the ref's decision and he was a cheat. The opposing team were deeply embarrassed; their team captain at half time apologised and added, "He's always like it."

Mr Wharton made his reappearance at half time. By this time the wind and rain had abated.

"OK boys."

"Where you been, sir. That fucking wanker is cheating like fuck." Houghton was really pissed off.

"What's happened? I only went for a smoke," Mr Wharton asked.

The boys explained and Mr Wharton nodded but his hands were tied.

The second half was much the same. Portsdown scored two good goals, both disallowed by the ref. Despite Mr Wharton getting involved, the result remained at 1–0.

"We'll have that bastard!" Raff and Hazer had copted. So they got changed as quick as they could. There was only one car in the car park so it had to belong to the caped crusader cheat. Hookey kept watch while Hazer and Raff crept over to the car and let all four tyres down. The team formed at the bus stop.

Back on the bus, as it drove by the playing fields they could see a disgruntled teacher kicking the front tyre of his car. The boys had pushed the windows of the top deck of the bus down with their heads stuck out. All you could hear was, "You fucking cheating wanker", with the wanking motion coming from their flaying arms.

The caped crusader looked up at the disgruntled Portsdown lads but couldn't hear what they were shouting as the wind and rain had returned, but he recognised the wanker gesture and clenched his fist as he waved it through the rain-sodden air. The boys couldn't hear what he said but if a lip reader was among them he would have read his lips saying "I'll have you, you little bastards".

So Monday morning back at school, the bell rang into assembly, nothing unusual.

Mr Digby the headmaster, after the prayers and God stuff was over, addressed the school.

"We have been let down," he pronounced. The boys, all 500 of them, wondered why. Hazer was among the clueless.

"Our football team." He took a long breath. "The Portsdown football team." He paused. "Has let this school down so the members of the team will report to me in my office after school."

Hazer, Raff, Upsall, Ray, Harding and the rest of the team were puzzling all day. What was wrong?

The bell rang 4 o'clock the team waited at the bottom of the stairs which led up to Mr Digby's office. Mr Palmer came down the stairs. "Boys, you can go up now." The boys still didn't have a clue. Hazer thought because they were top of the league they were going to get a pat on the back but on entering the room the pat on the back turned into a whack on the arse. Behind Mr Digby stood the caped arsehole crusader. The atmosphere turned from bad to bad, bad, bad.

Hazer's hairs stood up on the back of his head but he knew he had to behave or it was back to Glen House. Raff was fuming. Hazer could see Houghton's fists were so tight they were blue.

"I've had a complaint from Mr…" Hazer never heard his name, to him it would always be 'Fucking Cheat'.

"I believe," Mr Digby carried on, "that one of you let Mr Fucking Cheat's tyres down, so I'm giving you the opportunity to own up or this football team will be disbanded."

Hazer turned to Raff. They both shrugged. Upsall grinned. Hookey laughed. Simmo smirked. Jacko shrugged.

So the whole side had the detention. No one was grassed at Portsdown Academy For Young Gentlemen.

We lost the league by one point and we never played again for our school.

The flicks

The boys were too old for Saturday morning flicks so when a good film was on, i.e. preferably a war film, the gang would club together to raise the ticket money so one of them, preferably an older gang member, could pay then after the lights went down, sneak to the emergency exit which was usually next to the bogs (toilets).

So it was Sunday afternoon, the boys gathered outside the Palm Court, a posh cafe. The cash was handed to Corrigan. "Give me 20 minutes and I'll open the back door," adding "Remember, be quiet." He was looking at Teddy who was always laughing.

The boys disappeared down the side alley. Nobody had a watch, so 20 minutes seemed like an hour.

Micky had paid his entrance, had his ticket torn in half by the doorman (you had to keep this half to prove you had paid but most customers, once seated, dropped the stub onto the floor).

Micky, after the lights went down, made his way to the gents. The emergency doors were opened, six early-teenage boys crept in. "Be quiet," Micky put his fingers to his mouth, adding, "remember, one by one."

So the boys crept to the main door of the cinema (which was lit by the gents sign) so the only way to enter was to open the door just enough so you could crawl in, so the usherette couldn't see them. It was like The Great Escape but in reverse.

The boys crawled across the cinema floor till they reached a row of seats. The rule was don't sit together until the lights went up, after making sure you had picked up a stub end of a ticket to prove you had paid.

The lads successfully deployed around the cinema. The trailers were over, the lights were up. Hazer stood up, looked around, waved to Raff and Erky who stood up and joined him on the row Hazer had chosen was empty. Plummy then joined them. By the time the main feature was on, the whole gang was settled down in one row. They had broken the rule.

Taffy the bouncer had noticed the boys' movements. He came down the aisle with the usherette, her torch leading away. He tapped Plummy on the shoulder. "Ticket," he ordered. Plummy fumbled in his jean jacket pocket then produced a scrumpled up stub. He handed it to the Taff with a cheeky grin on his face.

Taffy inspected the ticket then asked to see Hazer's who had anticipated and had his ready to hand over. The only trouble was Hazer's ticket was the wrong colour. Every day, ticket covers were changed.

"It's the wrong colour."

"What's the wrong colour?"

"Your bleeding ticket."

Plummy interrupted, "I told you they never clean this fucking fleapit." With these words he was doomed. Taffy grabbed him by the scruff of the neck. Hazer stood up, "Why don't you pick on someone your own size?" Plummy was taller than Hazer. Taffy was at least a foot taller than Hazer.

Taffy threw Plummy to the floor then hit Hazer with a right hook, knocking him back in his seat. The rest of the gang piled on Taffy rendering him safe. They made a dash for the exits, all going in different directions. Hazer ran for the ladies exit, accompanied by Austin. Taffy couldn't chase all of them so he gave up, brushed himself down, recovered his composure and resumed his position at the rear of the cinema.

The lads would learn a lesson from this episode. Never sit together.

They bunked in both the Essoldo and Odeon many times after this but because it was dark when Taffy had nabbed them he never recognised the Bunkeriners on future visits.

The strike

Monday was back to school, but at assembly Mr Digby had an announcement to make. "Quiet," Mr Palmer shouted. The boys ceased chatting among themselves, as Mr Palmer took no prisoners.

Mr Digby cleared his throat, adjusted his tie, pulled at his coat sleeves.

"Good morning, gentlemen," sang out from the stage.

The boys replied in mumbled muted voices, "Morning sir."

"I have some grave news," he opened, carrying a stormy look on his face.

Johnny thought someone had snuffed it.

"Some boys have accosted a young lady from the senior girls school. This happened during Friday lunch break. Under the subways (the subways went under the dual carriage way)."

Johnny and his mates started to whisper amongst themselves, wondering who and what had happened.

"The boys in question have been dealt with by the police, but the reputation of Portsdown has been sullied." Johnny thought sallied? Who the fuck is Sally?

Mr Digby continued, "So I have had a meeting with Mrs Turner, head of Portsdown Senior Girls, and we have agreed that because of this incident starting times and leaving times will be staggered so the girls will not encounter any boys on their way to and from school. So you're starting times and going home times during lunch break are this – you will stop at 12:15 and be back at 12:45. Is this understood?"

The school went silent. The older boys didn't like it at all.

No more standing outside the school gates, chatting up the birds as they passed to go to Portsdown Senior Girls. A lot of the boys had to stay for school dinners, others had to rush home, have lunch, and rush back. So missing a quarter of an hour was pushing it.

The school was awash with disgruntled 13- to 15-year-old tempers, so at playtime, some groups started to form.

"He can't do that!" Austin was on his soap box.

"He's fucking done it," Hazer swore. He had just realised what girls were for.

The older boys of 4A were milling around outside the toilets grumbling away.

"We'll get a petition," John R. was heard to say.

"Hazer," JR called out. "Here a mo," he added.

"What's up, John?" Hazer asked as he joined 4As lads.

"You and Austin, get your year to sign. Them we'll get year one and two to sign."

So it was agreed this was a democracy. Austin was good with words so he made up the document.

The document read:

We the undersigned pupils of Portsdown Senior Boys here by contest the staffs' alteration of starting and finishing time during dinner 'hour'. (Please note the word 'hour')

We the undersigned believe we have the right to stick to present starting and leaving times.

We await your agreement on this matter, or we will have no option but to take industrial action.

Delegation representing the boys.

J Ralph
D Johnson
E Johmsey
J Hayes
M Austin
M Rafferty

This was drafted onto several pieces of foolscap paper. Hazer, Austin, Raff from the third year went about getting the signatures of pupils from the second year and third year. Everybody signed. J Ralph (JR), Erky, Plummy, Ronnie J, Eric Johnsey dealt with fourth year and first year pupils.

A count was made and out of 520 boys, 480 had signed either by free will or with a little persuasion.

Ralphy, Hazer, Erky, Jommsey, Austin, collected the papers up.

"Right, what we gonna do now?" Hazer inquired.

"We'll draw cards, lowest card gets to take it to Digby," Johnsey suggested (there was always a card scheme going on in the cloakrooms). As luck would have it, Austin drew a deuce (two) the lowest as ace was high so he had to take the petition to Digby.

"I ain't going on my own," he protested and he was right. He would most probably get the cane and the document would be torn up and thrown in the bin.

The boys thought their objections were within their rights as some weeks before in history the Tolpuddle Martyrs were the subject matter. How they stood up to their oppressive landowner, the farmers were the forerunner of the unions (that's what Mr Palmer, history teacher, quoted) though they got shipped to Australia for their protests. There was no way they could ship 500 Portsdown senior boys there. The thought rushed through Hazer's brain as he and the delegation knocked on Mr Digby's door. They knocked again, the door squeaked as it was opened. The school secretary stood in the doorway holding a stack of papers to her breasts.

She smiled as she asked what the delegation wanted.

"We're here to see the head," JR said.

"Have you got an appointment?"

"No, but we have a petition," Austin butted in.

"A petition, whatever for?" The secretary asked, a puzzled look on her face of thick make-up.

"About our times, miss," Jommsey piped out.

"What about your times?" Thick make-up asked.

"We – and I speak for the majority of the school – think it's wrong we have to alter our school hours, to suit the girls school." Austin had his diplomatic head on.

"Oh my, do you want to see the head?"

"That's the idea," a sarcastic voice sang out.

"What's all this?" came from behind the gang, who turned in unison to see the intimidating figure of Mr Digby.

"A petition, sir," the spokesman muttered.

"A petition?" roared the head.

"Yes, sir," someone said from the crowd.

"What's it about?"

"The times," Austin stood his ground.

"That's a newspaper," came Mr Digby's sarcastic reply.

"No sir, our school times." Austin was not for bending.

Mr Digby shook his head. "Let me look at this petition."

Hazer held out the papers for his inspection. He browsed the ink-stained papers, the odd tut coming from his lips.

"Leave this with me," he finally said.

Phew. Hazer thought they were in deep shit but Mr Digby shushed them out of the way and entered the office, dismissing the gang.

Some days went by and no mention of the petition was forthcoming so it was decided by the delegation an approach would be made to Mr Digby. So after assembly they gathered at the bottom of the stairs leading to the head's office.

"What are you doing here?" Mr Wells asked.

"Waiting for Mr Digby," someone answered.

"What for?" Mr Wells was puzzled.

"Our petition," another voice from the crowd.

"Oh that." Mr Wells smiled, adding, "in the wastebasket."

"Sir, I must protest, that was a genuine document." Austin was on his high horse again.

"Just go to your classes before any more of this stupid nonsense spreads."

"It's not nonsense. We have a real grievance." JR was coping the needle.

"Look, if you don't go to your classes, I'll give each of you detention." Mr Wells was losing his patience.

The group mumbled amongst themselves. "They have asked for it," came out loudly from the middle of the scrum. So the next day the word went out after lunch break. When the whistle goes to return to class, everybody is to sit down and not move – a sit-down strike. Never heard of in the history of schooling.

The whistle went. Four-hundred and eighty pupils sat on the playground floor. Poor Mr Farrow (music teacher) and Mr Groves (taught anything) were bemused.

"Get up and go to your classes," Mr Groves shouted. The boys remained seated, talking amongst themselves as if the teachers didn't exist.

"Get up now!"

The boys ignored the order. It was as if they were older.

"Go and get the head," Mr Groves ordered Mr Farrow, who by now was visibly shaking.

Mr Farrow knocked on Mr Digby's door. "Come in, what's up? Farrow, looks like you've seen a ghost." Mr Digby laughed at his white-faced visitor.

"They won't get up."

"Who won't get up?"

"The boys."

"What bloody boy?"

"All of them."

"All of who?"

"The boys. The whole school." Mr Farrow was flummoxed. Mr Digby shook his head, went to his cupboard, and retrieved his persuader. A four-feet long bamboo cane.

"Right, follow me, Farrow, I'll show you how to deal with this."

He charged down the stairs, flung open the double doors which led onto the playground.

He cast his eye around the seated strikers.

"I'll give you one chance. Go to your classes now," he raged, his face bright red, his veins appearing above his brow.

"Nobody move!" somebody shouted out.

Nobody did move.

"Farrow, get every master and make sure they have their canes," he ordered. Mr Farrow, who was not a disciplinarian and hated the bamboo, left the scene.

The bald-headed prince of darkness stood slapping his bamboo against his hand.

"One more chance or I'll cane the lot of you."

Some boys were starting to bottle it, whispering amongst their peers.

"Don't give up. We have our," Hazer shouted, making sure Mr Digby was looking the other way.

"Rights. You don't have any rights," he retorted.

A couple of minutes past, then the doors onto the playground started to open, disgorging 15 or so puzzled teachers, each armed with the Punisher. They approached Mr Digby who gave them orders. They then surrounded the boys.

"Last chance!" Mr Digby shouted.

No movement came from the strikers.

"OK, pick out the ringleaders!" he shouted.

The teachers started to strike the students willy-nilly across their backs.

"Ouch, Ouch. Ouch," was to be heard all over the playground.

Some boys, seeing the treatment meted out, stood up before they could be hit and ran to the safety of the classrooms. But the hardcore never gave in, despite several whacks across the back. Mr Digby was starting to wilt, knowing he was all but breaking the law.

"OK, enough. I'll listen to your complaint if you go to your classrooms."

Nobody moved. Jommsey set the tone. "Don't give in, he's lying."

After about an hour, the school playground was starting to feel hard and damp on most of the remaining hardcore strikers' bums. A name count was carried out by each form master on Mr Digby's instructions.

Another 30 minutes passed. The teachers had given in trying to bully and control the remaining boys back to class. They stood in small groups, puffs of smoke rising above their heads. Mr Digby had disappeared back to his study. After ten minutes, he reappeared, carrying the petition and the declaration of Portsdown Senior Boys rights as seen by the self-appointed delegation. The bald-headed avenger held up the document with one hand, slapping it with his bamboo equaliser held in the other.

"This is not a true reflection of my pupils," he shouted. "You all know I'm a fair man and I'll listen to your complaints."

The boys shuffled on their backsides, which were going numb, whispering among themselves.

"Do you reckon he's gonna listen?" Hazer asked his group.

"Dunno," came the general reply.

"Well, my assholes gone fucking numb," Houghton whispered, adding, "I don't care if we get the works. I'm pissed off and I'm gonna piss myself. I'm breaking my neck for a leg."

As Hazer looked around, he could see several boys on the brink of peeing in their pants, each one holding on with the look of anguished gargoyles on their faces.

"So, if the boys who organised this sit-in come to my study we can discuss our differences. I promise to look into your complaints."

The delegation stood up and met in the middle of the seated lads

"What you think?" JR questioned his accomplices.

"I reckon he's telling the truth," someone said, the rest of the delegates nodded. Some muttered, "Suppose so."

"OK gentlemen, if you would be so kind as to go to your classes." Mr Digby spoke in a calm and dignified voice. The boys stood up, most of them automatically rubbing their bum cheeks to get some blood flowing into the numb flesh. Some made a dash for the outside bogs to relieve themselves of the copious amounts of fluid in their bladders. Hazer was one of those. He just made the urinal, a queue forming behind each lad who was lucky enough to be nearer to the brick-built (cold as hell in winter) toilets when the strike began.

Hazer shook his manhood (well, nearly) and returned to his class. Mr Evans entered.

"Well, 3A. You are supposed to be the cream of the school, but of all the classes on this misguided endeavour you, yes, you, you, you." He pointed to several of the boys. "Had more boys per class than any other." He shook his head in disappointment. In fact, out of 38 boys in 3A, 32 had withstood the pressure till the end of the sit-down strike.

Mr Digby was true to his word. He made a speech at the next assembly, which rescinded that timetable. So it was back to normal time. He added he would trust the gentleman of Portsdown to behave during the lunch hour. Deep down, Hazer thought Mr Digby must have somehow admired the stance his boys took on that damp October day.

The surprise package for Mr Wells

It was all silent as the boys of 3A bent over the English exam paper. The occasional 'what's an adjective' whispered to the boy next to them. If an answer was not forthcoming, a note was passed around under the desks, but Mr Wells was a teacher who had sixth sense, a bit like a cat who never missed an untoward movement, so in nine out of ten occasions the note was intercepted and the culprit held in detention after school. Didn't matter who sent the scribbled note, the recipient always got the sentence.

So a plan was devised to thwart Mr Wells and give the lads a good laugh.

"Right, hold on to this." Austin held out a sheet of schoolbook-sized lined paper. On top in capital letters was 'NOSEY PARKER'. Upsall held it out, Austin proceeded to pick his nose and place the contents in the lined paper.

"Who else got one?" Upsall laughed, as his finger dived into his nose. Hazer always had a snotty nose so a large dollop was added. Simon, Hookey and Faithfull all contributed to the pile of gunge. When Austin had enough, he carefully folded into a 3-inch square booby trap. The bell went and the gang re-entered the classroom, the wooden chairs awaiting the backsides of the reluctant pupils.

The test resumed. Silence. Mr Wells looked up from his desk to see Hazer giggling.

"Hayes, what's funny?"

"Nothing sir."

"Well get on with your paper." With that, Mr Wells went back to his reading.

Austin whispered across the aisle to Faithfull, "Pass it on." Faithfull dutifully passed the folded paper on to Simmo, Houghton was next, then it was handed on and on until it was purposely dropped by Upsall who made a pretend scramble to retrieve it.

"What's this then?" Mr Well's face had caught Upsall red-handed.

"Not mine, sir. Must have flown in through the window. It's really windy out there." Upsall always had an excuse.

The boys all looked out of the wood-shuttered glass window. The winter sun was shining, not a puff of wind made an entrance to the tree-lined playing field on view.

"Bring it here, Upsall."

"But sir, it ain't mine."

"I don't care whose it is. Bring it here now."

Upsall picked up the note with his back to Mr Wells, a broad grin on his face. The rest of the class were trying not to giggle, some lifting the lids of their desks to hide their clowned lipped faces.

Upsall turned back to Mr Wells. "Bring it here," Mr Wells was beckoning Upsall with a bent finger on a closed fist. Upsall placed the note on the desk. "It's not mine," he pleaded, standing in front of the class. Mr Wells proceeded to unwrap the note in a dramatically deliberate manner.

"We'll see what's so funny, shall we 3A?" As he opened the last fold, a look of utter disgust took over his face. The words 'NOSEY PARKER' was smothered with large green runny bogeys. He automatically dropped the paper snot holder to the floor. "You little b…". But he stopped himself from swearing.

The class erupted in laughter.

"Detention, all of you!" he raged before regaining his composure. "Pick it up Upsall and put it in the bin."

Upsall obeyed, keeping his head facing the floor so his

smile could not be seen by Mr Wells. "If you were to put more effort into your work instead of practical joking…" he stopped mid-sentence, shook his head and resumed his seat. "Carry on with your exam paper," was the last word he said until the bell went and it was time to go home.

"I thought we had detention, sir," Polly asked.

"Just get out of my sight," came the reply.

The club (Hillside)

Johnny made his way home, calling into his gran's house on the way. He bounced through the back door. His gran was busy, her back bent over the copper boiling up the clothes. The copper stick, which he had felt a few times in his younger years, was busy being whirled around inside the copper, a pair of tongs by the side ready to lift the clothes out and put through the mangle which stood guard by the kitchen door.

"Hello, what do we have here?" his nan said.

"Alright, Nan," Johnny blurted out.

"Haven't seen you."

"Sorry Nan, been busy, you know school and that."

"Go and say hello to Granddad"

"Ge'uss us a cuddle first." Johnny gripped his nan round her waist.

"Get off, you silly sod," she shouted but didn't try and resist Johnny's greeting.

"Is that you, our Jon?" came from the front room.

"Yes Granddad."

"Come sit down."

So Johnny sat down next to the boot polisher extraordinaire.

"How's school, been behaving?" he questioned.

"Yes, gramps," he lied. Only a white lie.

"Tell us what you been up to, then."

"Not much, just school stuff. Footy, Hillside." He never mentioned the strike.

"What about boxing?"

"Nah, I gave it up."

"Why?"

"Messed with my footy," Johnnie shrugged, adding, "Anyhow, can't train for both."

"Suppose you're right," Gramps said as his lifted Boomer's brogues up to add an extra buff.

"We're going down the club later," Johnny said. "It's good down there, loads to do," he added in an excited tone.

The fire was spitting out bits of nutty slack. But the warmth of that and sitting on the arm of the chair with his grandpa doing his thing, was the most comforting feeling Johnny ever had in his younger years.

"What's the name of that club again?" his granddad asked.

"Hillside, Gramps. It's down Cheltenham Road. It's for snooker tables, table tennis tables, darts, loads of other things."

Johnny couldn't wait to get down there, but had to get the cash. So the plan was to wait till one of his uncles came home from work and play the poor, destitute waif.

So to pass the time he sat on the sofa which was occupied at one end by Kathy (his disabled sister) listening to the radio, and chatting to her, even though she couldn't talk back. He held a two-way conversation for her, her smile lighting up the room when he told her about the bogeys in the notepaper.

The door to the kitchen opened. Harry filled the entrance. His blond curly locks down to his ears, red rosy cheeks, which had been buffeted by the cold winds on the building site where he earned his living.

"Hello Harr." Johnny's look was both warm and sincere though his inner thoughts were 'here's a shilling'.

"Alright our John?" Harry said as he put his knapsack on the table, the contents of which he had eaten during his work breaks – spam or cheese sarnies, sometimes if he was lucky corned beef.

Without Johnny having to plea, Harry put his hand in his pocket, drew out some coinage, checked through with his fingered other hand and produced a shiny shilling bit.

"Here you are," Harry smiled.

"Thanks Harr." Johnny grinned, taking the coin and burying it deep into his school trouser pocket. Johnny repeated the innocent pauper when Boomer made his entrance – another shiny shilling hit his outstretched palm. Only Lenny to come.

Lenny came in, his bicycle clips still attached to the baggy dockyard trousers he wore, day in, day out the same pair. His face was as red as a newly fired wall brick from his exhaustive cycle journey home from the dockyard gates, which he had contested the exit of with 4,000 other dockyard men bearing bicycles, each clawing through the streets surrounding the dockyard. If you were unlucky and got your bike wheel stuck in the tram lines that were everywhere and fell off, you would be trampled by the dockies' rush for freedom. This had happened to Lenny on several occasions in the past.

"Hello Len," Johnny cheerfully greeted his last cash-bearing uncle.

"Let me get in!" Lenny was having his usual moan as he bent over to remove his bike clips, allowing his baggy trousers to bellow out

"Want me to put your bike in the shed?" Johnny was on the creep. Lenny never answered but continued to remove his shoes.

"Bloody hell your plates don't half throw up," Boomer said, automatically holding his nose with two fingers.

Johnny ignored the pungent aroma. He didn't want to upset Lenny and risk losing a tanner (sixpence). Lenny didn't earn as much as Boomer or Harry, so Johnny didn't mind a reduction. Lenny stood warming his hands by the open fire, rubbing them furiously to try and get the blood circulating again after gripping the handlebars on his five-mile journey from work in Portsmouth's Royal Dockyard.

"Well, better be going," Johnny called out as he reached for the rear door.

"Behave!" his nan said, shaking her sweat-filled brow, the exertions of the washing and steam from the copper boiler adding to the heat in the kitchen.

"I will Nan, honest!" Johnny knew his nan worried about him. She had read it in the tea leaves that he was a wild card. His nan always read the tea leaves, a bit of a clairvoyant or Gypsy Lil.

Johnny crossed the road and green, the front door of number 9 Dersingham Close was ajar. He bounded in like a cat after a mouse.

"Mum what's for tea?" he called out, not caring as he wasn't really hungry and he wanted to get ready for the club.

"It's in the oven," Jeannie, his younger sister, said as she looked up from the kitchen sink where the dinner plates wallowed in the soapy water.

"You can wash your own plate," she added. She hated doing the washing up. Johnny, being a boy, was excused all women's duties, but he always made his bed up.

He opened the oven door to find the plate of mince and totties swimming in a gravy of fat. Johnny's mum couldn't cook but Jock loved mince and totties. So for four days a week that was on the menu. Johnny screwed his face up as he removed his mum's signature dish from its hiding place, placed it on the kitchen table, nibbled a spud, then emptied the remains into the bin before his mum called could find out.

"He' are, Jean," he said as he plunged the empty plate in the washing-up bowl. The remaining gravy floating to the top of the flat water.

"Wash your own plates."

"Your job."

So Jeannie reluctantly resumed her job, muttering obscenities under her breath. She was 11 years old with a stubborn mind of a grandmother.

The door to the front room was shut. It was always shut to keep the heat in from the coal fire, the only source of warmth in the house. He opened the door and bent his head round. The family were watching *Children's Hour* on the 12-inch screen of the black-and-white television which sat in the corner of the room. His mum looked up on hearing the door creak open.

"Have you ate your tea?" she questioned (she thought her cooking was perfect as Jock never complained).

"Yeah Mum, going over the club."

"Dad's left a bob on the sideboard."

Johnny reached for the shiny piece of metal, adding it to the coins in his pocket.

"You better tidy your room first."

Johnny's room was a teenage room, comics, fag cards, bits of everything but under his mattress was a copy of *Titbits*, a magazine with ladies in their underwear. That's why he always made his bed up before going to school.

"Alright Mum!" he chirped.

So after a quick tidy up, the strip wash was next, so into the bathroom, door secured, Johnny stood in the bath and washed his nether regions as vigorously as he could. He was on the pull, a good scrub under his arms, where a bunch of hairs had accumulated, a good scrub of his bits, which also carried a smattering of hairs.

He looked in the mirror to check if he could grow a beard, but all there was were one or two lonely hairs on his chin, but taking Jock's razor, he shaved his hairless face. After foaming it up with Jock's shaving brush and special tin of soap, next came Jock's Brylcreem. A dab on each fingered hand, rubbed furiously into his jet-black hair.

After this ritual, he returned to his bedroom, pulled on his ice blue jeans (still never had underpants), his shocking blue socks, followed by his suede Chukka boots. The shirt followed then the latest fashion (he had pleaded with his mum so she bought one with the Provi cheque), a mohair jumper (not real mohair) coloured mauve, was pulled over his head. He felt the coolest schoolboy of all time. The hair was next, carefully combed with the duck's arse at the back and the Elvis quiff. He looked in the mirror. The club was his oyster, the girls wouldn't be able to resist this icon of Portsdown Senior boys.

He was ready. Just one thing was missing – his shoelace necktie – so a furious search ensued until it was found under the bed. The last piece of style was applied. He was ready. The comb he always carried was pushed into the rear pocket of his jeans, ready to be drawn like a gunfighter at the OK Corral if his hair dropped out of place.

The gang were waiting by the shop – each one of them in pristine condition, ready to pull a bird – so they headed down the hill to their girl-filled destinies.

A large queue was formed outside Hillside Youth club. The girls chatting amongst themselves, the boys trying to look hard. The occasional shoulder shrugged the neck muscles taut as they combed their slick-backed hair. Ernie stood in the doorway, nodding to each teenager as they paid the entrance fee. He was a big man, broad shouldered, a ruddy face, a cauliflower ear from his boxing days, a pug nose, a cigarette held in his hand. Johnny noticed the hand had only four fingers, including his thumb. This was to puzzle Johnny for years until all was revealed in a football match against a team from Germany many years in the future.

The Friday dance

"That's one and six," Peggy, Ernie's better half, asked each paying customer. It was a Friday and every Friday a live band was playing. That's what brought teenagers from different areas of Pompey to Hillside and it was Johnny's first time.

Johnny and his mates entered the dimly lit club. The band were busy setting up the equipment the old 'one, two, one, two' coming from the stage. Johnny always thought it odd they never got to three.

Finding a seat was next priority. They had to have a base to meet after strutting their stuff on the dance floor. The trouble was Johnny couldn't dance, never tried. He was too shy. His older mates had been to the club, so he watched their approach to the dancing girls. The girls seemed to dance on their own in bunches of three. One girl in the middle and two girls dancing around her. It was called the jive.

Johnny was stood, back against the wall watching, hoping that one of the ballerinas might notice him in the darkness.

"You look lonely," a voice whispered in Hazer's ear. Hazer was taken aback as he turned to look at the Whisperer. Hazer gulped as he answered. "Alright." Johnny's heart was racing. A young lady of a more mature age had just talked to him. He was flummoxed. "Do you mind if I stay here?"

"Na, why should I?" (The scarf came out.)

The band played, but Hazer was still the wallflower. But with an older admirer. The band played on then it was the interval.

"Do you fancy going outside?"

Fuck me! Hazer's heart nearly left his rib cage. He pursed

his lips trying to look at least 15, shrugging his narrow mohair-carrying shoulders

"Yeah, alright."

So this sophisticated girl, some five years older than Hazer, led him out of the club. She led him around the back of the flats that overlooked the club. Hazer had never kissed a girl. His escort grabbed his hand and put it on her breast. The explosion in Hazer's sky-blue jeans was like Mount Vesuvius' explosion in Italy 2,000 years ago. Her lips engulfed Hazer's like two suction pumps. Then he felt a tongue inside his mouth. Bollocks, he thought he was choking. His mind was racing, his heart was beating, his penis was about to do something it had never done.

"Alright," she said.

Hazer didn't know what to say.

"Better get back."

Shit. Hazer had just fallen in love and she wanted to go back to the club.

The time back to the club was spent in utter silence. Hazer never even knew her name.

"Where the fuck have you been?" an 18-year-old teddy boy asked as he grabbed Hazer's older companion.

"Just went for a walk," she replied as she turned to wink at Hazer. The older lad looked over her shoulders towards Hazer who was trying to melt into the background. He must have been suspicious, but having weighed Hazer up, he shook his head. "What you looking at?" he directed the question to Hazer who shrank back. "Nothin," he replied, trying not to arouse the teddy boy's anger. What he really wanted to say was 'I just snogged your girlfriend', but he bottled it, and 'she put her tongue down my throat' he wanted to add but discretion being the better part of valour, he kept his gob shut.

Back in the dancehall, the place was buzzing. Girls

twirling round, petticoats flying like multicoloured discs, the odd stocking tops showing a suspender belt; the boys, some dancing, taking two girls jiving to the beat of the rock music.

"Where you been?" Teddy asked.

"I just snogged some bird," Hazer smiled.

"Yeah, pull the other one," Teddy rebuffed.

"Honest mush," Hazer crossed his heart.

"Yeah alright, which one?" Teddy was curious.

Hazer looked around the packed dance floor. There in the middle, dancing with her teddy boy mate, was the tongue-in-throat.

"Over there." Hazer moved his head and eyes in the direction of the dancing couple.

"Fuck off." Teddy didn't believe a word Hazer said, but Hazer would never forget his first proper snog.

The dance went on, the boys looking to pull a bird to walk home when it finished, each trying to look the part, combing their locks into place, a cigarette dangling from the lips, the smoke going up their noses making their eyes water, but they had to withstand this inconvenience to look hard.

Hazer never smoked, so he had to think of something to make him stand out. The answer was a Coca-Cola bottle. Instead of holding it as normal people did, he concocted a new method by placing a bottle in the palm of his hand, gripping the bottom of the bottle, then placing the open end to his mouth. He thought this was sure to get him noticed.

The lights went up after the band had finished. This was another enigma Johnny could never figure. The band would announce the last song, sing it, go off stage, wait for the crowd to shout' more, more', come back onstage, take another bow, play the same song again, go off stage, wait for 'more, more', come back onstage, bow, play the same song again. The singer always saying, what a great audience you have been.

This could continue for three or four encores. Hazer could never figure out why they just didn't carry on playing instead of wasting time going off stage and making an entrance of coming back.

So the lonely journey back up to Wymering, no young lady to escort home. But next week maybe Hazer would get lucky. Hazer put his hand through the letterbox and retrieve the front door key, which was attached to a piece of string on the back of the door. No problems with burglars in those days. As he opened the door, the noise from the front room hit him. Jim Reeves was singing on the gramophone, accompanied by a drunken Jock and his mates. Johnny pushed the living room door open. Bottles of beer were strewn about the lino-laid floor. Five of Jock's mates were pissed as farts, all singing out of tune to 'Put your sweet lips to the phone', the words of a Jim Reeves song.

They all turned to Hazer as he opened the door. The smell of alcohol hit Johnny in the face. The boozed-up assembled gang muttered a welcome. "Come on have a beer," one of them said, holding a bottle of brown ale out towards Johnny.

"Nah. Got to be up early for footy," Johnny said as he closed the door.

Portsdown Hill

Johnny was up like a lark, donned his footy gear and two-sizes too big tracksuit. He grabbed a bit of toast, a cup of milk, then was on the corner waiting for Raff when a young girl of his age said hello. Johnny was a bit taken aback as no girl had approached him first before.

"I'm new here, just moved into. Number 28," she said a smile lighting her face.

Johnny answered, "I live over there," pointing to his house on the green.

"What you doing?" she inquired.

"Going to footy down the jube." Johnny was trying to look as if he always had birds chatting him up.

"Hazer, who's the bird?" Rafferty had come up behind him.

"My name's Irene. I'm not a bird," she retorted, then asked, "What's your name then?"

"I'm Johnny or Hazer. This is Mick or Raff." Johnny was getting up his confidence.

"Come on," Raff said, adding, "We're gonna be late."

"See you later," Irene said with a broad smile on her face

"Yeah, sure." Johnny smiled back.

"She had some knockers on her!" Raff held his hands to his breasts as if he was holding two large melons. Hazer just laughed.

So it was down the hill on their bikes as fast as the wind. The game was much like any other league game. No incidents as before down the common.

Sunday morning came. It was freezing as Johnny drew

the curtains. The ice was on the inside of the panes of glass. He shuddered as he looked out to see four inches of snow covering his back garden.

Johnny quickly got his togs on, had a quick rinse of his face in cold water (no running hot water), cleaned his teeth, which had a gap in the front courtesy of Taffy's right hook.

"Going over Nan's," he shouted upstairs to his mum who never replied.

The smell of booze engulfed the house. Jock had had his mates back again.

As he opened the front door, the cold, refreshing air hit him. It turned his face a rosy red colour. He took a deep breath. The freezing air said hello to his lungs. He gave a brisk 'brrrrr' then bounded out into the white carpeted street kicking the snow like he would a football.

"Hello Nan, it's been snowing," a grinning red face said as it opened the kitchen door wide.

"Close the bloody door, I'll catch my death!" his nan announced, giving a cough from her cigarette-dangling lips.

"What's for breakie?" Johnny was as hungry as a horse.

"I'll do some porridge. That'll keep the cold out."

Johnny never answered, as he joined his granddad in the front room.

"Alright, Gramps?"

"Bloody fire won't light. Wood's got damp," his gramps answered. Sure enough, the fire was struggling to take hold, so it was time for a page of the sketch to be applied to the open fire to draw the air up the chimney, thus acting like bellows igniting the kindling. The fire started to roar. The sketch caught on fire, Gramps still holding it as the flames burned his hands. Johnny, grabbed the paper and put it out in the grate before it could do any more damage.

"What's going on in there?"

"Nothing, Nan."

"You alright, Gramps?"

His granddad looked at Johnny, wrinkled his eyebrows and nodded.

"It snowed last night, Gramps."

His granddad peered out the window and nodded. "What you up to?" he asked.

"Gonna make a sledge go up the hill." Johnny sounded excited; he loved the snow. That was until he was wet and freezing to the bone. After a large bowl of porridge and a slice of thick buttered toast, Johnny left his nan's to call on his mates, ready for the Winter Olympics of Portsmouth.

The gang assembled at the bars outside the paper shop, each carrying a hastily built sled, all made from odd bits of timber pilfered from garden sheds, most of which were ex-air raid shelters, Andersons, that is.

Portsdown Hill was ideal with runs of 200 yards before you ran straight into the back lane, which ran along the bottom. It seemed the whole of the local kids from six years to 17 years were ploughing the slopes, the odd cry of pain echoing out as some daredevil over did it and ended up in a bush or hit a snow-buried tree stump.

The light began to fade as the happy-faced sledgers started to thin out, each heading for the sanctuary of the warm firesides which glowed in the front rooms of the council house estates of Portsmouth North.

The barber's tools

The Christmas holidays were over. It was back to school. Johnny had got his head down and was working hard as he had promised after his little adventure in Glen House. But sometimes he just couldn't help himself going off the rails. The assembly hall was packed, 480 mostly unkempt boys, most wearing hand-me-downs or clothes from the rag and bone man. This was a poor area but the camaraderie among each age group was second to none.

Mr Digby took the stage. "Morning gentleman, he spoken in a loud, authoritarian tone.

"Morning sir," came the mumbled reply of his captive audience.

"Welcome back, I hope you had a nice break."

The boys mumbled, "Yes, sir."

"Somebody left me a Christmas present and I forgot to take it home with me."

He held out a parcel wrapped in Christmas paper. "I'm afraid there was no label on it, so would my benefactor like to stand up."

"What's the benefactor?" Simmo whispered in Hazer's ear.

"Dunno, I think it's the mush who sent it."

"Well, gentlemen, I thank you, whoever you are," Mr Digby said as he began to open the parcel. The box appeared. It was in an old shoe box. He lifted the lid and peered inside. He looked up to the schoolboys, looked back in the box, then gave a brief tut and nod of his head sideways.

He lifted an item out of the box. A comb with no teeth hung between his thumb and forefinger. The school at once burst out laughing. Mr Digby was bald as a badger. He replaced the comb and extricated a hairbrush, minus the bristles again. The school erupted in laughter. And finally, a hand mirror with no mirror was held up by Mr Digby, who had a furrowed brow above his reddened cheeked face.

"That wasn't expected, boys." He reverted from gentlemen to boys when he was flummoxed.

"I must say I've had better presents." Then a large grin came over his face. He shook his head from side to side.

"Gentlemen, you have had your fun, now it's back to work. Dismissed!"

"Who sent him that?" Hazer enquired of Erky as they left the hall.

"Think it was Johnsey and Kimber," Micky A replied.

So it was back to the desk until the weekend of freedom.

"What you doing tonight?" Micky asked.

"Got footy practice after school."

"No, after that. You going down the club?"

"Ain't got no dough," Johnny answered.

"I got enough. Our Jackie gave me ten bob," Micky A smiled.

"Alright, see you up the bars," Hazer said.

So after training Johnnie rushed home to get changed into his cool gear after checking under his arms for BO, cleaning his teeth with the two missing from the bottom front row (he went to get false ones but walked out) care of Taffy the Bouncer.

"Don't be late," his mum called out.

Johnny never replied as he closed the front door.

Weekdays in Hillside were quiet compared to weekends. Ernie was on the door as usual, a cigarette held in his one-finger-missing hand.

"Evening Ern." Hazer smiled as Micky paid their fees for the week. Ernie pushed the door open. The boys ambled in trying to act like 16-year-olds. Micky had started to smoke so he looked the part; Hazer couldn't stand smoke.

The rest of the gang were leaning against the wall watching a couple of birds trying to play table tennis. The ping pong ball bounced up near Simmo who caught it.

"Can we have our ball back, please?" a pretty young thing asked.

"Only if you give me a kiss." Simmo puckered his lips expecting a smacker. He got a smacker alright. The young lady whacked him round the chops with the table tennis paddle. This was a tough environment and the boys had to learn and learn quickly to blend in.

Then a 16-year-old teddy boy joined the gang. He had curly hair, short sideburns, large lips, and a grin as big as an airship.

"Alright boys," he chirped. The boys nodded back.

"Fancy a game of five-a-side out the back?"

"Yeah alright," Raff replied.

"My name's Lenny, by the way," his large lips uttered. "You boys new here?" he added.

"Yeah, only our second week." Hazer nodded as he stood up to follow Lenny out the back.

The five-a-side pitch was illuminated by two floodlights attached to the rear of the club. The pitch was tarmac with white lines marking the playing area, two small goals, one at each end, with a half circle surrounding each one.

"I thought you said five-a-side," Simmo said.

"Well, sort of whoever-wants-a-game aside," Lenny laughed. It was 12-aside or more, each boy kicking the crap out of each other, more like a rugby scrum than a football match. The only rule was he couldn't score inside the half circle around the goals.

The game carried on for an hour or so. It might have started with 12-aside, but because of the brutality of the tackles, it ended up more like 5-aside. Jonny and Raff managed to dodge most of the heavy attacks on their ankles and gave as good as they got in revenge over the top tacklers. Ernie had wandered out the back to witness the carnage, and was surprised to see Hazer and Raff holding their own with the bigger lads.

"That's it. The lights are going off," he shouted.

"Winning goal!" someone shouted, the war started again. The darkness left them groping for the ball.

"Well, what you think," Lenny asked.

Hazer lifted up his jeans to reveal a large bruise on his shin. "I got him back." He smiled as he rolled his jeans back down. Another couple of older lads, joined them, laughing about the tackles they had delivered on their victims.

The winter months dragged on; school was much the same. The only thing was a science lab being built on the end of the school block and the flats being built along the link road. Great fun could be had jumping off the scaffolding into the sand. And getting chased by the nightwatchman.

Erky always was mad about cars, so off he went to become a mechanic. Teddy joined the Canda clothes factory as a presser. Johnny always wondered what a presser actually did, but he couldn't be bothered to ask Teddy, so it was to remain a mystery. Plummy went to work in Goodwillie's Woodyard, which was situated at Flathouse Quay, stacking wood all day. Ronnie R. went to work with his brother Freddie on the building sites laying floors.

The American car

It was getting dark. The boys had started to drift away after a night at Hillside. Johnny and Teddy were by the bar drinking strawberry milkshakes from a carton, care of the new milk machine outside of Philbrows grocery store. For a tanner, you could get a pint of strawberry, raspberry and any other berry milkshake ice cold, which was a new experience, as nobody had fridges in the early 60s. Most drinks were warm except in the middle of winter.

Johnny had just guzzled the last drop down his parched throat when a Hooter made him regurgitate the last mouthful all over Teddy's knew Chukka boots.

"Sorry Ted, that fucking hooter make me jump," Hazer apologised, wiping the drips from his mohair jumper.

"Who the fuck's that," Teddy said as he turned to see a large American car, its headlights illuminating Peterborough Road like the floodlights at Fratton Park.

Hazer looked at Teddy and shrugged his shoulders.

"Oy, fancy a ride?" A voice came from the half wound down window.

Teddy and Hazer looked at each other. Both had a puzzled frown etched on their faces.

The window continued to be lowered, then a blond curly head emerged. "You comin' or not?" Erky laughed.

"Fuck me Erk, where you get this?" Teddy inquired as he smoothed the bonnet.

"It's part of my job. I'm a mechanic, just giving it a trial run. You fancy it?" Erky smiled.

So the boys jumped in the front bench seat. Hazer had

been in Jock's car but this was something from the future. It had knobs upon knobs, a radio which they couldn't get to go, air conditioning, a column change for the gears, luxurious leather seats which Hazer could smell was real leather and it was left-hand drive, that's why Erky was able to lean out the window on the wrong side.

So the tour began around Paulsgrove, Porchester down the back lanes, back to Wymering. Then just as the joyriders passed the Clacton pub, this great beast spluttered and died. The boys found out later it had ran out of petrol.

"Fuck me. What's up, Erk?" Teddy exclaimed.

"I don't know," Erky shrugged.

"Thought you was a mechanic," Teddy laughed.

Hazer had to giggle at Teddy's sarcastic remark.

"Come, you'll have to help me push it."

"Where to?"

"Back to the garage."

"Where's that?"

"Stamshaw."

"Fuck off, Erk. That's miles away."

"Come on, let's try." Hazer jumped out and started to try and move this five-tonne lump of American engineering. Teddy joined him but they couldn't budge the joyrider's giant. Erky was halfway out the door trying to push and steer, but it was impossible.

"We'll have to leave it, Erk," Hazer said. "Sorry, mate."

"But I got to get it back tonight," Erky pleaded.

"Get it back to where?" a deep baritone voice echoed behind the gang.

They turned around to be confronted by two of Her Majesty's finest constables.

They made a grab for Hazer and Teddy, but the two boys were as quick as a rat up a drain pipe. They bolted the first garden fences and disappeared into the darkness, leaving poor Erky to take the wrap. Nobody grasses in Wymering.

It turned out that Erky had borrowed the keys from his workplace. It wasn't to check out the car as he said, it was for a joyride. So he lost his mechanics job and his licence, which he never had, cos he was only 15 and you can't drive in England till you are 17. Hazer and Teddy, after a long roundabout trek through the back gardens of Wymering to avoid the bobbies, made it back to the sanctity of Peterborough Road.

"Phew, that was close," Hazer panted, his thoughts on the promise he made to his nan and granddad to behave.

Teddy was bending over trying to catch his breath. "See you tomorrow. I'm knackered," he said, as he walked up his path, pulled the stringed key from out of the letterbox, opened the door and disappeared. Johnny pushed his front door open as it was always on the latch and entered the hallway.

"That you, our Johnny," his mum called out.

"Yeah mum. goodnight." He crept into his room, lay on the bed, and drifted off.

At the club the next night. Ronny R. was asking Teddy what happened. Teddy was explaining the little adventure but adding a few porkies about how they'd escaped the rozzers. Teddy carried on exaggerating about the chase, how they'd outrun the police over the rear gardens, leaping the fences like an antelope, the police hot on their tails.

The truth was they didn't want to get their uniforms dirty and they had Erky so they could get the names of his accomplices out of him. They never knew Erky. He kept stum. It was then that Erky joined them.

"What happened Erk?"

He shrugged his shoulders. "Kept me in all night, fucking freezing in them cells. Questioned me, I told them you were helping me bump start the car." Case closed. Johnny let out a sigh of relief.

The loss of innocence

"What you lot up to then?" Miss X asked.

Rolphy, Hazer, Plummy and Austin were on the corner, deciding where to go – over the hill, rabbiting, taking pot shots at pigeons and pheasants with their weapons, air guns, catapults, etc., or down Cosham to bunk in the flicks.

"Can I come?" she asked.

"Only if you show us your tits," Plummy laughed.

"Piss off, you wanker." Miss X was quite indignant in her reply but the boys knew Ronnie had had them out the week before up his alleyway.

"Alright, no need to be like that." Austin was trying to placate Miss X. He put his arm around her shoulder and squeezed her. She smiled back. They decided to visit the hill with Miss in tow, after promising her they would behave.

The sun was beating down as the gang climbed Portsdown Hill. A bead of sweat was dangling from Plummy's nose as he removed his shirt, exposing a skinny white ribbed body.

"Put your shirt back on. You'll frighten the birds," Raff laughed.

Plummy flexed his biceps trying to imitate a bodybuilder.

"Look at this body. Don't you want to have it, Miss X?" Plummy said, the grin engraved on his face.

"No thanks," Miss X retorted.

"What, you don't find me attractive?" Plummy laughed.

"No, I don't, you wanker." Miss X had seen enough.

Hazer took his shirt off, striking the same pose. "What about me?" he said, a broad grin on his face.

Mis X leant forward and grabbed Hazer's nuts. He gasped

as his appendage grew to its full length, nearly bursting his jeans.

"Come on, Hazer. Let's see what you got," Miss X laughed, a cunning smile of devilment filled her round rosy-cheeked face.

Hazer went a reddish-purple colour, a look of 'fucking hell, she wants me' lit his face.

"Go on Hazer, give her one," the boys chanted.

Hazer recovered from the shock, smiled at Miss. Miss X smiled back. "I was only joking," she said.

Hazer felt a great weight lift off his shoulders, then Miss X turned to Raff. "Let's have a butchers at your cock." A mischievous grin filled her face

Raff's face smiled the smile of the devil. He wouldn't back out.

"Yeah, what you gonna do if I do?" he said.

"I'll give you a wank." Miss X called his bluff.

But she never knew Raff like the lads did.

As Raff started to undo his zip, Miss X wished she hadn't started the wind up.

"Not here, let's go behind the bushes," she reluctantly said.

Raff didn't need a chaperone. He was gone.

The lads waited anxiously then a loud 'ahhhh' came from the bushes.

"That didn't take long," Plummy laughed.

"Come on then," Miss X said, grabbing Hazer's hand, pulling him behind the bushes. The shock hit Hazer's brain like an ice cream brain freeze. Miss X unzipped his ice blue jeans, extracted his half lazy lobbed appendage, looked at it as the doctor would, then began to stroke it till the mushroom-headed beast arose to full length. Miss X smiled at Hazer, then whispered in his ear. "Don't tell the others," as she lowered her ripe, moist lips over Hazer's mushroom. It was like scoring the winning goal in a cup final. Hazer seemed to melt.

"Fuck me!" he exclaimed, as he reached the end of this wonderful journey.

Austin, Plummy and the rest of Portsmouth must have heard Hazer's first encounter with the devil.

"Your turn." Miss X grabbed Austin.

"Bloody hell," Miss X gasped as she viewed Micky's tackle. "That's a big'un," she added.

Micky was a big boy as the lads knew from the wanking competitions they held every now and then.

Then it was Plummy's turn. A broad grin lit his face as Miss X dragged him behind the bushes.

Miss X laughed. Plummy started laughing then a "fucking hell" was heard as Plummy reached the forbidden tree in the Garden of Eden. That's when birds nesting, rabbiting took second place to girls. Johnny's only goal from that moment on was the pursuit of the Holy Grail between a girl's legs.

The lab

The new laboratory was completed; the boys were to be its first occupants. This shining new classroom was a beacon of the future. The old Victorian desks replaced with state-of-the-art furniture. Each desk had a gas outlet for the Bunsen burners. The teacher had a small platform with his desk replaced with a lectern. The blackboard was reversible, behind which the walls were covered in glossy posters, describing everything from the solar system to the deepest oceans and their fishy inhabitants.

Hazer was pleasantly surprised at his new home. It really was a pleasure to be taught in such an environment.

Mr Evans began the lesson about the sun's rotation, earth, etc.

Hazer's mind drifted back to the last summer and the opening of the play park in Sevenoaks Road, swings, roundabouts, etc. But they were past all that. But it had a large turfed area ideal for football, but no ball games notices were hanging from the fence, so the parkie Jack, had to turn a blind eye. In fact, he liked a game, so he joined in running around like a young hare. Jack told Hazer he was in the desert during the war and he learned to tell the time by the sun. Hazer was a bit dubious, so Jack would look at the sun, study it for a minute, then tell Hazer the time and he was always correct. One day, Jack's peaked cap flew off whilst he was playing alongside the lads. Johnny bent down to retrieve it when he noticed trapped inside the hat the face dial of a pocket watch. So Jack's reading of the sun and time of day was a trick. Hazer thought that's why Jack always took his hat off, to shade his eyes when telling the time. He handed the hat back to Jack, a smile burst out of Jack's tangled mess of a face as he winked at Hazer, who winked back. He kept Jack's secret throughout his teenage years.

"You with us Hayes?" Mr Evans whispered in Hazer's ear.

"Yes, sir!" Hazer shouted. Mr Evans had crept up behind Hazer whilst he was having a reflective moment.

"Well tell us what we were discussing."

"Time, sir." Hazer had caught the words somewhere in his subconscious.

Mr Evans returned to the front to continue his lecture on time and the speed of light. The lecture dragged on, each boy having to write a short essay at the end.

It was a month or so later when the experiment went horribly wrong.

"Split into groups of eight," Mr Evans ordered. Mr Evans had spent an hour or so setting each test, tube beaker, etc. on the correct stands. A large bowl (size of a pint glass) was placed on the stand, the Bunsen burners underneath. Several glass tubes connected to test tubes. The large bowl had a coloured liquid in it. Mr Evans's instructions, as soon as the liquid changes colour turn the gas off. This was 3A, the cream of the school. Surely they would act sensibly. Wrong. Austin looked at Faithfull and Hazer as the colour started to change, Hazer moved his head from side to side. "No Mick," he said. Faithfull laughed. Then it happened – bang, the bowl broke. Shards of glass flying everywhere, some in Micky and Faithfull's cheeks. Hazer had ducked under the desk just in time as the next explosion occurred. Then a third experiment filled the room with glass. Several boys were cut by the glass. Mr Evans turned a vivid green colour. He went apeshit, so no more did 3A have experiments in the labs. It was bookwork only as they couldn't be trusted.

The school trip

"I've arranged for 3A to go on a trip to visit a Union Castle line cargo ship," Mr Bucket informed the class. The school had adopted a cargo ship which sailed between Southampton and the South African city of Cape Town.

"You will need to bring sandwiches as it's an all-day visit. Those who have school dinners will get a packed lunch from the dining hall," Mr Bucket explained.

The boys weren't taking much notice as Simmo was making suggestive movements behind Mr Bucket's back.

"Simmons," Mr Bucket shrugged.

"Yes, sir," Simmo replied, quickly placing his hands behind his back.

"Sit down and try and act your age." Mr Bucket had caught Simmo's actions in a window reflection.

"But sir..."

"No buts sir, Simmons or you'll do 100 lines." Mr Bucket raised his thick bushed eyebrows as he reprimanded one of the class clowns.

"We're going on a trip," Johnny informed his mum.

"That's nice," she replied, not looking up from the book she was reading.

"Got to take sarnies."

"That's nice."

"We're going on a ship."

"That's nice."

"To Africa."

"That's nice."

A thought went through Johnny's mum's head. "Did he

say Africa?" But she just returned to her love story of a book.

Johnny gave a sigh. "I will get Nan to make me some sarnies."

"That's nice."

With that, he closed the door and directed his size 5 Chukka boots over the road to his nan's house.

"Hello stranger," his nan greeted him.

A puzzled look came on Johnny's face. "It's me, Nan."

"I know it's you."

"Then why did you call me stranger?"

"It was sarcasm," his nan replied.

"Sarcasm? What's that?" Hazer questioned.

"I don't know, I heard it on the brains Trust [a radio programme]. Now what do you want? I'm busy." His nan was always busy.

"Need some sarnies tomorrow."

"What for?"

"School trip to Southampton. Going on a ship to Africa."

"Don't be daft." His nan gave a smile.

"Only kidding, Nan, but we are visiting a cargo ship that goes to Africa."

"Oh, what's up with your mum doing your lunch?"

"She's too busy."

"Busy doing what?"

"Reading a book."

His nan shook her head. "Come over in the morning. I'll have it ready."

"Thanks, Nan," Johnny shouted as he vanished again, just like the cat in Alice in Wonderland.

The next day after roll call and assembly, Class 3A gathered at the school gates.

The coach arrived. Johnny and most of his mates had never been on a real luxury coach, with proper upholstery and blinds to keep the sun off. The only time Johnny had been on the coach was Royal Navy wooden seated.

"Get at the back!" Austin shouted.

So a scramble started till the gang had the rear bench seats and the nearest coupled seats.

The journey to Southampton was quite a trek (no motorways then), passing through Portchester, Fareham, Swanwick, Lordshill, then Southampton. The docks were packed with ships of all sizes, but one stood out. The *Queen Elizabeth* was massive.

As the boys left the coach, the size of this magnificent ship seemed to overwhelm them.

"This way. Follow me," said a merchant seaman, who was dressed in a uniform much like a petty officer in the Royal Navy. The boys ambled behind the seaman. The gang who were last to alight the coach some way behind the main group.

"Keep up at the rear!" Mr Pearson shouted, but the order fell on deaf ears as the boys were busy talking amongst themselves. The trail led the boys through the large warehouses filled with all sorts of goods that had been unloaded by the stevedores. The place was buzzing with men pushing handcarts and sack trucks, loading lorries with the cargo which was landed in great nets from the dockside cranes. No containers then. That was when a broken crate was spotted by Micky.

"Let's have a butchers," he said as he knelt down making out he was doing his laces up.

A smile came over his face as he held up a large yellow ball-shaped fruit, a melon. The boys hadn't seen such a fruit before. Micky threw the yellow ball at Hazer who automatically trapped it like a football, then gave it a whack to Upsall who gave it an almighty boot. The contents of the melon sprayed the rest of the gang with mush. Bits of yellow mush littered the floor.

"What's going on?" a loud voice boomed.

The boys looked around to see a large pug-nosed stevedore with not a happy look on his face standing behind them. The boys took one second to recover, then took to their heels, leaving Mr Pugnose to clean up the mushy mess.

"Keep up boys," Mr Bucket said as the giggling boys joined the end of the queue at the bottom of the gangplank.

"Follow the first mate. He's going to be our guide, "Mr Bucket shouted so he could be heard above the noise of the dockside.

The tour started with the engine room. Johnny was really impressed with the size and the cleanliness, brass and copper polished to an inch of perfection.

Then the hold (where cargo is stored). This was huge. It was like being inside a giant tin can in Johnny's mind. Then the bridge, the captain's domain.

The boys filed past all the various instruments, each function explained to the school boys by the first mate. Then the crews' quarters. As the boys entered, the view that greeted them took them by surprise as the walls were covered in graphic glossy photographs of naked young ladies all striking different poses.

"Whoa, she's got some knockers!" Upsall called out. His classmates joined in the banter. "I'll give her one!", "Look at the arse on her!" and several other phrases that in today's world would be seen as derogatory to women.

"OK. You have seen enough." Mr Bucket was quite embarrassed. So instead of having the packed lunch in the crews' mess, the class had to sit on deck munching away, now and again, throwing lumps of crusty bread into the air for the seagulls to sweep and fight over. Johnny had enjoyed the visit, and in his mind a life in the Merchant Navy was not a bad thing if he never made it as a footballer (which of course he would, that was his belief – as you know, it never came to be, but that's life).

"Back in the bus, sit in the same seat," Mr Pearson barked.

The gang resumed their places at the rear. The teacher had done the roll call. One missing. It was Upsall, as usual, always late.

"Where is Upsall?" Mr Pearson inquired.

"Having a pee, sir," Simmo answered.

"Where is he having a pee?"

"Up the side of the bus."

The boys looked out the windows and there he was releasing his fluids against the rear wheel.

Mr Pearson tapped on the window. Upsall looked up and mouthed the words, "breaking my neck, sir", a grin all over his face.

"Hurry up," Mr Pearson mouthed back.

The journey home began.

"Guess what I got?" Simmo whispered to Hazer.

"What you got?" Hazer answered.

With that, Simmo pulled out a magazine from up his jumper. He had nicked it from the crews' quarters. Micky had heard the conversation.

"What's in it?" he asked.

Simmo held it up. It was a pornographic magazine. The wording was in a language the boys didn't understand, but the pictures were very, very graphic. Simmo began to tear pages out of the mag and distribute them among his mates. The coach was not travelling at a great pace, but the driver was getting flustered by all the overtaking vehicles who kept sounding their horns as they passed. Some drivers or passengers waving their hands and pointing to the rear of the coach thinking he had done something wrong, he pulled over to the side, opened the coach doors and went to the rear of the bus, checking underneath the tyres, the rear lights, etc. Then he looked up at the rear windows to be confronted by pictures of naked ladies in compromising positions plastered across the windows. He smiled and thought to himself, boys will be boys. He re-entered the coach, whispered in Mr Pearson's ear, who stood up and walked to the rear and joined the boys.

"What's in the windows?"

"Don't know, sir," the boys chorused, trying not to laugh.

"Well take them down and give them to me."

"What, sir?" Austin pleaded.

"The nudes."

"Is that what they are, sir?" someone answered.

"Yes, that's what they are," he exploded.

So the boys handed over the porn. Mr Pearson returned to his seat and 3A never went on anymore school trips.

Betrayal for nookie

It was a Friday night. The boys were at the bar after a night out at Hillside, when the conversation turned to Miss X, who they had been talking to that night.

Micky opened with, "Do you reckon we can go round her house tomorrow? Her mum and dad are on holiday."

"Yes, I suppose so," Raff answered.

"What time should we meet?" he added.

"Dunno, 9 o'clock."

"Alright." They all agreed 9 o'clock.

"Here," Plummy said. "I've got to tell you this."

"Tell us what?" they asked.

"Well, you know the other day up the hill?" he continued.

"Yeah."

"Well, you know when we gotta wank?"

"Yeah."

"Well, she told me not to tell anyone, but as you're my mates, I've got to tell you."

"What?" The gang were all ears.

"She told me not to tell, but she gave me a blowjob." Hazer looked at his mates. In turn, they looked at each other.

"She told me not to tell anyone," Hazer uttered.

"And me", "And me," they all reiterated.

So each boy thought he was the special one.

Then Plummy gave a "Agh!"

"What's up, Plum?" Micky asked.

I only snogged her," he exclaimed.

"Fuck me, so did I," Hazer admitted.

Micky A nodded but didn't say a word.

Raff laughed his head off. "So did I," he said.

But the boys knew he went first, so it didn't count. They each made a vow, no snogging Miss X in future.

The next day, Hazer was up at 7 am. The sun was shining. He was looking forward to visiting Miss X.

"You've got football?" his mum asked.

"No, mum, season's finished."

"What you up so early for then?"

"Going out with me mates."

"This early?" she asked with a puzzled expression on her face.

Hazer didn't answer as he didn't want to lie to his mum. He did his ablutions, taking extra care to wash his private parts and double cleaning his teeth. His hair was treated to some of Jock's Brylcreem so it stood up in the Elvis style. He brushed his suede Chukka boots, put on his best shirt and mohair jumper. After pulling up his ice blue jeans, he was ready.

"Miss X, here I come!"

"Don't you want any breakfast?" his mum asked.

The smell of bacon in the pan was something Hazer couldn't resist. He hesitated, then thought about Miss X, then about bacon and would his mates wait for him.

Bacon won. He took off his mohair jumper – he didn't want egg yolk to get on his best clobber – threw it back in his bedroom, then joined Jock at the kitchen table.

"Alreet, son?" Jock greeted Johnny with a mouthful of black pudding (care of Uncle Bob in Glasgow) being more than enjoyed.

"Yeah, I'm starving," Hazer said as he sat opposite his dad. A plate of bacon, eggs, black pudding, beans and fried bread was placed in front of him, all swimming in grease. Hazer attacked the plate like a man possessed, making sure he didn't drip any on his ice blue jeans or his best shirt. Jock carried on munching, taking the occasional slurp of tea from his pint-sized mug.

"You want a cuppa?" his mum asked.

"I'll have a glass of milk," Hazer answered.

Milk was off the menu years before, but Jock had landed a cracker of a job and money seemed no object anymore. So his mum poured Hazer a glass of milk in one of the many pint glasses Jock had borrowed (nicked) from one of the many pubs he frequented.

Hazer quaffed the milk down, then left a clean plate, after scraping a piece of bread around it to lap up all the greasy juiced bean sauce.

"Thanks, mum," Johnny said as he left the kitchen, re-entered his bedroom, checked his teeth in the mirror, pulled on his mohair jumper, and re-styled his hair in the Elvis mode. He was about to leave when, "Here, son," Jock said in his broad Scots brogue. Jock handed Hazer a fistful of coins, all silver, the change from the many visits to the bars of the previous night.

"Cheers Jock!" Johnny couldn't wait to count out his cash windfall.

As he slammed the front door behind him, the cash tingling in his pocket, he made his way to Plummy's house. It was just past 9 am.

"Hello, John." Plummy's mum had answered the door.

"David in?" Johnny always called Plummy 'David', his proper name, in front of his mum.

"No, he went out about an hour ago." She seemed puzzled.

"An hour? We were supposed to meet at 9 o'clock," Johnny said.

"Could have been more than an hour, in fact."

"Alright, I expect he's over Raff's house." Johnny waved as he left Plummy's front garden.

"Is Michael in?" Johnny asked, as Mrs Rafferty answered

the door. He always called Micky or Raff 'Michael' in front of Mrs Rafferty.

"No, John, he went out about 7 o'clock. I thought it was a bit early," she answered, adding, "Have you got a game today?"

"No, seasons finished," Hazer said.

So the visit to Austin's house with the same answer. He had left over an hour before. The boys had done the dirty on Hazer. The reason was Miss X. So Hazer left Wymering and made his way to Paulsgrove, where Miss X lived.

He crept up the garden path, lifting the letterbox. He peeked into the hallway of Miss X's house. He could hear voices, his mates' voices, and Miss X talking about doing it!

Hazer knocked on the door.

"Shhhh! Be quiet," Miss X whispered. "It might be my big brother."

Hazer knocked again, lifting the letterbox. He shouted in his deepest voice, "Open this door now!"

Miss X crept to the window and looked out to see Hazer laughing his head off. The gang had left the building through the back door and were hiding in the garden shed.

Miss X open the door. "You bugger. You scared me to death!"

"Where are they?"

"Hiding In the shed."

Hazer went to the shed door and banged his fist on it as hard as he could.

"Come out, the games up," he said in a deep baritone voice.

They opened the door somewhat reluctantly to be confronted by Hazer with a big grin on his face.

"Thought we were meeting at 9 o'clock?" Hazer asked.

"Don't blame me," Raff said. "I was a little bit early but I couldn't sleep. I got here at 8 o'clock and Plummy and Micky A were already here."

Plummy piped up, "Yeah we was a bit early. I met Micky at the shop when he was paying his mums' bill. He said let's go round early, it won't hurt. Micky added, "I know we was early but we got here at 7 o'clock and Simmo was already here, the wanker."

So the gang of true friends would, for the sake of a bit of nookie, cheat on each other but they stayed friends for life and the stories of Miss X and that day would be repeated into their retirement.

Philbrows grocery store

The boys still loved visiting the back of Portsdown Hill and the Yankee Woods in particular where GIs were camped before D Day, in the grounds of HMS *Dryad*, where the Operation Overlord was planned. So it was decided to camp at the stream over the weekend so provisions were needed and that meant visiting Philbrows grocery store. When Peter was minding the shop, the boys planned to go in one at a time. Teddy entered, Peter quickly handed him four packets of Birds Eye beef burgers (a new thing in England), which he stuffed down his shirt. Re-joining the boys, "Got beef burgers," he said.

Ronnie R went in, came out. "Got the tins of beans with sausages in." Erky got bacon which Peter had wrapped in greaseproof paper as bacon was cut on site in a special bacon slicer from a full side of bacon.

Plummy returned with beans, Raff with packets of Walls sausages. Hazer's turn; now Peter, who could have a nosh, loved Kraft cream cheeses which came in a round flat box, 12 cheeses to a box, each one shaped as a triangle with a rounded top. Hazer was partial to these little delicacies too. He entered the shop. Peter was behind the counter smiling. He always smiled. "Quick!" he said as he handed Johnny six boxes of cream cheeses.

Hazer struggled to stuff them down his duke (Scotch for jumper) as he only had his old one on which was too small. He was getting taller.

As he turned to exit the shop, he heard voices at the top of the steps which led down to the shop entrance. It was Gilbert, Pete's dad, and Pete's mum, who was a very imposing woman.

Peter was starting to panic. "Get out," he whispered. As he disappeared behind the counter, Hazer tried to act casual as he passed Peter's parents on the steps.

"Morning Mrs Philbrow," he chirped.

"Strange," Mrs Philbrow thought to herself, "what's young Johnny Hayes up to this early in the morning?"

As she reached the bottom step, the alarm bells were ringing. "What you got up your jumper?" she shouted.

Hazer was on the top step. "Nothing," he said.

He took flight across the grass of Deal Road. "Come back here now!" Mrs Philbrow shouted, so loud you could have heard her a quarter of a mile away.

"Can't, got to meet my mates!" Hazer turned and called back. Mrs Philbrow shook her fist, "Little buggers been thieving. I'll get him next time!" The next time Hazer encountered Mrs Philbrow a few weeks later, as he had kept his distance, she gave him an almighty whack around his lughole, which he deserved. It was better than calling the police, Wymering and Paulsgrove justice! And it worked as Hazer never took anything more from Philbrows grocery store again.

"Phew! That was close!" Hazer exclaimed as he met the gang up Ronnie R's alleyway.

"What you got?" someone asked.

"Bloody Kraft cheeses," Hazer answered.

"Don't like them."

"Nor do I."

"Nor me." The gang were all agreed.

"But Peter does," Hazer put his two penneth in.

Johnny Hutchings stood at the top of the steps leading to Ronny R's alleyway. He later joined the police force.

He was laughing as he joined the gang.

"You've dropped something, Hazer," he said, holding out a single cheese. In fact, Hazer had left a trail of cheeses across

Deal Road green. One of the boxes had come open and 12 delightful Kraft cream cheeses adorned its grass, standing out like silver triangles on a Christmas tree.

After an hour or two, Peter joined them ready for the camping trip. All the boys carried Bowie knives (not as a threat) though a game they used to play was a bit dangerous. You stood with your legs apart and took turns to throw your Bowie knife to stick in the ground as near to your opponent's boots as was possible till someone chickened out. As the knife got closer, you had to close your parted legs a little after each throw.

"Stop throwing that fucking knife," Peter shouted at Ronny R who was aiming to miss Peter's sandal-clad foot.

Ronny laughed. "What's up, don't you trust me?"

"No. I fucking don't." Peter was getting angry.

The boys marched on up Portsdown Hill. Ronnie couldn't help himself. He had to wind Peter up. All of a sudden, Peter gave out an almighty scream. The boys turned to see what was up. Ronnie was white as a sheet, his eyes popping out of his eye sockets told it all.

"Fuck me, Pete, Raff said. "Does it hurt?"

"Course it fucking hurts!" Peter screamed.

The rest of the gang stood motionless, gazing at Peter's sandal-clad foot with a six-inch Bowie knife embedded in it, the blood oozing out down his sock and disappearing into the downtrodden grass footpath.

"Want to go to hospital?" someone said.

"Fuck off," Peter replied as he drew the knife out of his foot, making the blood gush out onto the footpath. With a mighty throw, he hurled Ronny's knife into the bushes.

"What you do that for?" Ronnie asked all innocently.

"You fucking wanker," Peter swore. "I'll fucking kill you."

"Don't be like that. It was an accident," Ronnie pleaded.

The rest of the gang were trying not to laugh as Ronnie protested his innocence.

"It just slipped out of my hand, honest." Ronnie was panicking.

"Yes and into my fucking foot too, you tosser." Peter's face was red with rage

"Calm down Pete. It's only a scratch." Erky tried to take the pressure off Ronnie.

"A scratch? It's a fucking hole!" Peter was still fuming.

"That's it, then you going home, or what?" one of the gang said.

"Yeah, I'm going home and I'm taking my grub with me. That's it, then, the camping's off."

So the boys turned around and started the trek home, Peter hobbling behind, cursing his head off. He needed loads of stitches when he went to the hospital.

Picasso

"We got art this afternoon," Micky informed Hazer as he was looking at the new school timetable.

"I don't mind art," Hazer answered.

"Bloody boring," Upsall, piped up.

"Stop talking and study the timetable," Mr Evans said.

The new timetable for summer term had been distributed amongst the class. As Hazer glanced through his copy, he noticed a free lesson on Thursday, one and a half hours.

"Any questions?" Mr Evans asked.

"What's free lesson, sir?" Hazer inquired.

"It's one of the head's ideas. You can choose whatever subject you want for that one and a half hours," Mr Evans informed the class.

The boys chatted quietly amongst themselves.

Then Austin put his hand up. "You Austin, what do you want?"

"Sir? Can we do any lesson we want?"

"That's the idea." Mr Evans shook his head because he knew this meant trouble. "OK, so in the space for the free lesson place your preferred option," he added.

The gang thought for a minute. What would be the cushtiest lesson where they could skive off? Then Simmo hit on gardening! What better way to spend 90 minutes, mucking about in the school gardens? Chasing the chickens, throwing stones at the fish in the school pond. So it was agreed, gardening would be placed in the free lesson square. The gang of 3A miscreants had made up their minds.

After handing in the timetables with the free lessons

squared filled in, Mr Evans gave a groan. "So it's gardening for ten of you, is it?"

His head shook again as he shuffled the papers. "I thought as you're the creme de la crème, science, maths or English might interest you, but no gardening it is." He shook his head again. He never did agree with the head over free lessons.

The morning passed and after a kick around in the playground, in the dinner hour, it was back to class and an hour and a half of art.

"Come in boys." Mr Pearson opened the door to the class who were lined up outside chatting amongst themselves.

The art room was just another class but a few easels were scattered here and there for the best artists to use. The boys took their seats in no particular order, as Mr Pearson was a laidback hippie sort of man.

"OK boys. Today I want you to draw anything you can see in this classroom."

Johnny looked about and thought he would draw Mr Pearson at his desk. Well, try to draw Mr Pearson at his desk. Mr Pearson handed out clean paper, pencils and black crayon and wooden boards.

"Clip the paper to your boards," he instructed the class as he demonstrated the process.

Some boys were allowed to use the easels (the class artists). Johnny's head was up and down looking at Mr Pearson and trying to convey what he saw onto the sheet of paper. After about ten minutes he looked over at Upsall. He was sitting looking out of the window in a world of his own. Time went by and Upsall was still gazing out of the window.

Johnny hadn't seen him put pencil or crayon to his paper. The time was getting on. Over an hour into the lesson and Upsall was still away with the fairies. Johnny was getting curious, so he made out to drop his pencil, which he kicked in

Upsall's direction.

"Sorry sir, dropped me pencil."

"Well pick it up," he ordered.

With that, Mr Pearson went back to the Penguin paperback book he had been reading during the whole lesson.

Hazer crept up behind Terry. "What you drawing?" he asked.

"It's a secret," Upsall replied.

"But I ain't seen you draw anything." Hazer was puzzled.

"I'm a quick drawer," Upsall laughed.

Mr Pearson looked up from his book and gave Hazer a stern look.

"Sorry sir, I found it under Upsall's desk." Hazer had made his excuses and returned to his own drawing of Mr Pearson reading a book at his desk. After another five minutes, Mr Pearson replaced his book in his drawer and addressed the class.

"Have you all finished?" he asked.

Most of the class had done their worst or best to destroy art for future generations.

"OK, put your names on the top of your artwork. I'll have a look and give you my opinion."

So the boys signed their work and handed their masterpieces to Mr Pearson as he walked up and down the aisles between the desks, collecting the drawings. A few comments came from his lips. Johnny was quite proud of what he had attempted to portray and sat back waiting for Mr Pearson's good reaction.

"Well, boys, I've had a good look at each drawing but master Upsall can you join me?"

Terry stood up walked the front of the class, a grin on his face.

Hazer thought, as did the rest of the class, that he was in for a bollocking for not producing a drawing. Mr Pearson lifted the sheet of white paper with 'T. Upsall' in large letters on the bottom. The class burst out laughing when they saw Terry's drawing of anything in class artwork. It was a circle with the numbers 1 to 12 and the hands of the clock. It must have taken him at least two minutes to draw.

Everyone was expecting Mr Pearson to blow his marbles, but he looked at Upsall and smiled. "Well, Mr Upsall, what's this?"

"Well, sir, I saw this programme on the telly about this mush called Pistachio and he done drawings like mine and they were loads of money so I copied him."

"Well done," Mr Pearson smiled again.

"That is what art is," he added, then went into a lecture about the different art forms, from Cubism to still life. So the next art lesson, a chair, a pencil, a door, were the order of the day from some of the boys, but Hazer enjoyed art, so he tried his best, though it wasn't up to much.

Gardening

"Those who chose gardening report to Mr Wharton in the annex," Mr Evans ordered.

So the gang of 3A miscreants walked up the slope to Mr Wharton's shed.

Mr Wharton stood outside the wooden shed which housed the gardening equipment, his hands on his hips, a pair of dungarees hanging from his broad shoulders.

"So you lot chose gardening?" was his opening foray. "Think it's going to be a doddle, do we?" he added.

"No, sir," Austin answered.

"OK, you four grab these shovels and clean out the chickens' coop," he ordered as he handed a shovel each to Simmo, Austin, Upsall and Hazer.

The coop was about 25-feet square with a mesh fencing surround about six-feet high. The chicken coop was about the size of a small car with a door and egg boxes at the rear. And it stank to high heaven.

"Fucking hell it stinks," Austin said, holding his nose.

Upsall just laughed. He was used to pigeon shit as he cleaned his loft out every week.

Simmo started to retch. "Cough it up, might be a gold watch," Hazer said. It reminded him of his granddads' greenbacks (phlegm) sizzling on the log fire. He wondered why his nan always said these words when his granddad had a coughing fit.

"OK, I want this place clear of chicken shit before the end of the lesson." Mr Wharton's vocabulary was broad and didn't miss out on the odd swear word or two.

The boys started to scrape out the hen house, Simmo still retching.

After about 20 minutes, a pile of chicken droppings mixed with straw was piled outside the hen house. Austin looked at Upsall, a dirty grin on his big-lipped face. Simmo was standing talking to Hazer, his face a white ashen mask, a smudge of his puke was left on his chin, the leftovers from his dinner, which was now mixed in with the pile of chicken turds.

"You alright?" Upsall inquired into Simmo's health.

"Fuck off. I ain't doing gardening anymore," he retorted.

Unbeknown to Simmo, Austin had gotten on all fours between Simmo and the pile of docdah.

Upsall was laughing as he placed both hands on Simmo's shoulders and gave him a gentle push. The momentum made him step back, encountering the crcuched body of Austin. He lost his balance and wallop, entered the chicken shit on his back. A crowd had gathered outside the coop ready to witness the carnage. Simmo was up like a shot, covered in the muck. He picked up a shovel and hurled lumps of chicken shit at all and sundry. Hazer got a lump in the mauler. Upsall tripped Austin and lay on the floor laughing as Simmo shovelled turds on top of him. Austin couldn't move as he was laughing so much so he got the same treatment. The gardening class were in hysterics as the shit fight continued.

"What the bloody hell is going on?" Mr Wharton was not amused. The four chicken-shit covered boys peered up, a look of innocence on their faces.

"Fell over, sir," Upsall said. "So did I, sir." "So did I, sir". Before Austin could add, "So did I, sir" Mr Wharton raised his right palm. "Be quiet."

So it was the end of gardening for them. No wonder Hazer never had green fingers.

"Join me in my classroom. You can wash in the sink." Mr Wharton seemed rather calm.

The boys thought they had rode the storm, after all Hazer, Upsall and Simmo were in his football team.

They had counted their chickens to soon.

"You will not be in my gardening team anymore."

"That's alright, sir, we don't mind." Austin was being cheeky.

Hazer gave him a nudge in the back.

"But I will give you something to remind you of your gardening experience."

"What, can we have a chicken egg?" Austin had to open his gob.

"I've got something better than that," Mr Wharton said as he went to the tall cupboard in the corner, opened the door and turned around holding a three-foot long bamboo weapon of mass destruction.

So gardening was off the menu for the free lesson. The next week, Mr Evans inherited the gang of four. As all the other classes were full for free lessons. Mr Evans addressed the class.

"Today we will continue to learn how to play chess."

The previous week, Mr Evans had started to teach the 'free lesson boys' the noble game, as he called it, so he continued to explain the rules – how a queen can move anywhere, a bishop, diagonally, etc. The boys were set into groups of four with one chessboard between them. Each team tried to follow the instructions of Mr Evans.

No one knew that Hazer had learned the noble game while a guest at Glen House remand centre and would lay in bed practising moves on his old chess set donated by his master and instructor at Glen House. Left hand playing right hand.

"OK. Have you got the gist of the game?" Mr Evans inquired. No one said a word.

Then Hazer put his hand up.

"Well, Hayes?" Mr Evans said.

"I think I got it, sir," Hazer answered.

"Well, let's see," Mr Evans said as he pulled a desk to the centre.

"Gather round boys," he said as he beckoned the class to surround them.

Hazer sat opposite Mr Evans.

Mr Evans picked up the black king and the white king and hid them in his fists.

"What hand, Hayes?"

Hazer touched Mr Evans' left hand.

He opened his fist to reveal the white king.

"Does that mean I go first?" Hazer inquired, making out he was a beginner.

"Yes Hayes. It means you go first." Mr Evans was thinking that Hayes hadn't listened to a word he'd said.

So the game began. Hayes moved his white porn two squares. Mr Evans countered with his black pawn, one square. Hayes moved his knight. Mr Evans moved another pawn two squares. Hayes moved his other knight. Mr Evans counted by moving his knight. Mr Evans was starting to realise something was not right as Hazer began to take his pieces one by one. Every move he made, Hazer had an answer. The boys were spellbound watching Mr Evans getting flustered as the game continued into an hour.

"You sure you've never played Hayes?" Mr Evans asked as Hazer set a trap for his queen.

"No sir, I'm a quick learner," Hazer replied.

Mr Evans looked at his watch. It was ten minutes to 4 o'clock. "OK, that's enough. Put your chairs back," he ordered the class.

"But sir, ain't you gonna finish the game?" Faithfull chirped.

"Haven't got time I'm afraid," Mr Evans stammered.

So the free lesson was never chess again, but Johnny went on to play in the chess club and enjoyed playing and still does. He had many an interesting game with Mr Evans.

Cross country running

PE lessons were great if you played rounders, footy, etc. but running up Portsdown Hill in the pissing rain was a no go. That's why Mr Cook (PE master who had a sadistic streak) always chose cross country when it was raining or worse. While he stayed in the warmth of his little office at the back of the gym, the boys were sent off to run from Portsdown School, up Sevenoaks Road, along Peterborough up Wymering Lane to meet the rolling hills of Portsmouth, Portsdown Hill, then straight up a steep incline along the top of the hill on the small, worn path past a small chalk pit dug in the side of the hill, above Harleston Road, about a quarter of a mile long, 600 yards wide into the hill and 200 feet high, then onto the larger chalk pit about twice the size of the first one. This was still producing lime for cement etc. into the late 50s. The old sheds etc. still lay derelict. The boys followed the path to the other side of this, then descended the hill, returning to the lower path at the top of Leominster Road, then back along to Wymering Lane, through the gorse-strewn undergrowth often disturbing nesting birds which hit the sky in a flurry of tangled wings, and returning to Portsdown School, whence they had come.

The boys dragged themselves around this circuit at least once a month, and every boy in 3A hated it. Mr Cook had one and a half hours of free time while his shorts-clad, plimsole-wearing (school issue black with an elastic strap to keep them on) prodigy tackled the foreboding Mount Everest of Portsmouth. The fitter boys, Hazer, Upsall and most of the soccer team, were capable of achieving the run at a good pace. But their mates, Austin etc. would walk most of the way chatting as they went, often coming back half an hour after the other boys.

"I fucking hate cross country," Austin swore.

Mr Cook instructed the class on the route once again. It was raining as usual. The sky was black, the hill covered in mist.

"I ain't doing it," Austin whispered to Polly.

Polly repeated Austin' words to Upsall and Hazer.

"I'm going to hideaway and join you lot on the way back down." Austin had a plan.

"But he'll see you through his binoculars," Hazer questioned. Mr Cook had a pair of very strong binoculars, navy issue. He would stand in the playground and count the boys as they topped the hill by the pylons which ran from the hill into Pompey.

"No, he won't, look how foggy it is up there." Austin was right, so the plan was laid. They would sprint to the top of Sevenoaks Road, duck into Hazer's Nanny Fry's garden at the corner of Peterborough and Sevenoaks, wait till the rest of the class went by, then join them on the return journey.

So it was off. Hazer, Upsall, Austin, Polly and Simmo sprinted as fast as they could up the Sevenoaks incline some 600 yards at one in ten. The rest of the class were amazed at the enthusiasm they were showing. At the top, they dropped in Hazers' granny's backyard, hiding behind the chicken shed. Some five minutes later the last boys had struggled past. Then they raised their heads over the top of the shed to be confronted by Hazer's nan.

"What's going on?"

"Morning, Nan."

"You're bloody soaking, get in that kitchen all of you. You'll catch your death in them clothes, they're wet through."

So the boys trundled into the kitchen where Hazer's nan made them a cuppa. After about three quarters of an hour, the first of the runners appeared. The boys waited for a gap, then joined the rest of the class for the trot down to school.

On arrival back in the gym, the boys made out they were knackered, puffing and blowing, complaining of a stitch, each one leaning over and trying not to laugh.

"Well done, boys," Mr Cook congratulated the classes. "Good running, even Austin has done a good time."

So the boys knew every time cross country running was in the rain and the mist was dormant on Portsdown Hill, Nanny Fry had a visit.

"Rounders today," Mr Cook announced to Class 3A. The sun was shining, the sky an azure blue with faint wisps of clouds standing perfectly still as if anchored to the ground by invisible silk cords.

"Lovely day for rounders, sir," Upsall, chirped. He always had a smile.

"Yes Upsall, top field everyone, at the double." Mr Cook seemed in a good mood.

"OK, pick teams," he ordered. Collingwood and Austin. So each boy picked their mates.

The rounders area was marked out. Each base had a large wooden skittle painted white.

Hazer always played as wicketkeeper for the school team so in rounders he automatically took the stance behind the batsman.

"Not there. Hayes. I'll be there for both teams," Mr Cook said with a smile on his face. Hazer thought, "Bloody hell, he's happy. Must have won the pools."

The game progressed, the boys enjoying the banter and the sunshine. Now after three balls, if you never hit one, you had to run to the first base no matter what. And more often than not, you would be run out. Collingwood was into bat. He missed the first two balls, so Mr Cook got brave and closed in to catch the ball and run out Collingwood. Well, after you either hit the ball or miss it, you must drop the bat on the floor.

Collingwood was determined to whack the third ball into the next universe. His face was grimaced, his concentration at 100%. The ball entered his zone. He took an almighty swing, missed it completely, but instead of dropping the bat it made full contact with the dark-haired catcher called Mr Cook. A loud thud echoed around the green, a loud 'agh!' came from Mr Cook's blood-soaked face. He went down like the proverbial sack of spuds, out like a light. His eyes were still open but he was sparked.

The boys stood gobsmacked. Collingwood's face was white beyond white. Austin started it, he giggled up. Upsall looked at Austin, as did the rest of Class 3A. The sort of worried looks was replaced with giggling. Mr Cook lay there. "Do you reckon he's alright?" someone spoke.

"Yes, he's a tough old git," someone else added.

Hazer and Upsall knelt down and peered into Mr Cook's blank eyes.

"Do you reckon he's dead?" Upsall looked quite serious.

"Nah. He's just sleeping," Hazer said, looking at the large lump growing on his cheek bone.

Then Mr Cook groaned.

"Told you he ain't dead," Hazer said.

Mr Cook's eyes started to water. He blinked a couple of times, then out of his blood-splattered mouth came the immortal words, "Don't panic, boys."

"We're not panicking, sir," Austin said.

"Did it hurt, sir?" came with sarcastic question from Faithfull.

"Course it bloody hurts."

Mr Cook tried to get up, but it was too much for him.

"Shall we finish the game, sir?" someone asked quite innocently.

"Go get a master."

"What master, sir?" Simmo questioned.

"Any bloody master."

So a master was summoned. Mr Cook made a full recovery and was back at school within a couple of days. But Hazer got his job back as wicketkeeper.

The visitors

There was a knock on the front door. Hazer stirred as it was still dark. Who could it be? Jock was sound asleep as were his mum and siblings

Bang, bang! Hazer shook his head as he crawled out of bed to answer the door.

"Alright alright! Hold your hair on, I'm coming!" he shouted as he opened the door of his downstairs bedroom. "Who is it?" he asked before opening the front door.

"It's us!" came a broad Scottish voice.

"Whose us?"

"Uncle Bob" came, the reply. The Scottish brogue was as heavy as a lump of lead.

Hazer opened the door and was faced with his uncle Bob and a young man who he hadn't seen for some years.

"Hello Bob, what are you doing here?"

"Just passing through," he answered, a smile on his reddened cheeks.

Well, the only place he can pass through Portsmouth to is the Isle of Wight, so Hazer gave a puzzled look.

"Who's that?" A voice came from the stair landing.

"It's me John." Bob always called his older brother John.

"What?"

"It's me."

"What you doing here?"

"Just passing through," Bob replied.

Jock had joined them downstairs in the hallway. Both gave him a hug. Jock shook his head knowing Audrey wouldn't be too happy.

"Passing through to where?" Jock inquired.

Both ignored this question.

"I'll put the kettle on," Hazer said, breaking the ice.

Jock and Bob started to talk amongst themselves. The young man joined Hazer in the kitchen

"You don'ee remember me?" he asked Hazer.

Hazer haven't seen Jim (or James, as he was christened) since he was nine years old. And then it was only for a day or so on one of his Glasgow visits. Jim had grown into a broad shouldered 5-foot-eight clean shaven teenager. His hair cut short, combed with a parting, his broad chin held two thin lips above it. Topped with a small upturned nose, blue eyes, thick eyebrows and a forehead built to batter. He had just been released from borstal and Bob, in his wisdom, thought bringing him to England would put him on the straight and narrow.

"How long?" Jock was heard to say.

"I'll be off in a couple of days," Bob replied.

"How's everybody, son?" Bob asked of Hazer. He always called him son.

"Alright, Bob," answered Hazer, a yawn leaving his open mouth.

Bob smiled as he clutched his mug of steaming hot tea.

"You'll have to kip in the front room till I can sort something out," Jock said. "I'm goo'in back to ma bed. See you in the morning."

"Who's that?" Audrey asked as Jock got back into bed.

"It's our Bob."

"What's he doing down?"

"Passing through."

"Passing through to where?"

"Go back to sleep! I'll sort it in the morning," Jock said as he rolled over and pulled the covers over his shoulders.

'Passing through' became a family joke over the years.

Jock was earning good money. He was a general foreman on a large building site called the Berg Estate, so he was in a position to get Jim into employment with the groundwork gangs into which Jim settled working alongside Boomer, Bernie White, Bertie Shaw and Hazer's other uncle Ronnie August. They worked hard and played hard at weekends.

The only bugbear was Hazer had to vacate his single room for his sister Jeannie and share a double with Jim.

"Fancy going over the new club?" Upsall asked Raff and Hazer.

"What new club?" Raff was keen to meet new ladies.

"Grove Club over behind the shops," Upsall answered.

"What's it like?"

"Brand new snooker tables, darts, table tennis, jukebox, you name it." Upsall was full of the Grove Club. "And a proper cafe."

"How much?" Hazer was thinking money.

"Only a bob."

So it was decided the boys would visit the Grove Club that night.

This wasn't like Hillside. It was all new furniture and equipment and it was run by the council. But it had loads of rules which Hillside didn't.

The new boys weren't welcomed as they had been at Hillside and they were in competition for the young ladies, and the locals didn't like it. The queues for the snooker tables were always long, sometimes over an hour or maybe two, but the boys stuck at it until one night when Jim accompanied them for a game of snooker. The boys had put their names down as usual and had joined Jim in the cafe where he had treated them to a real coffee with cream. This was a real treat.

"That's on Jim," Hazer said as he handed the coffees

round to his mates.

"Cheers mush," they replied. Jim nodded, not knowing what mush meant.

The lads were next on the snooker table when two teddy boys came in. They were dressed in drapes, tight trousers, white shirts, their hair immaculate, jet-black Elvis-style. Aged late teens/early 20s, but they looked hard and acted as if they owned the place. Everyone was keeping out of their way like they were the two princes of darkness in their dark, foreboding attire. They went to the snooker table, looked at the names on the chalkboard, then put their names to the top of the list. Nobody said a word.

Hazer said, "Did you see that?"

Raff turned round, as did Jim.

The two boys who were next in line didn't say a word, but Hazer and Austin were next after them.

The game was over. The two teddy boys went to rack up the balls when Jim got up, walked over and rubbed their names off the board, took the cue off the table and handed it to the next players.

"Who the fuck you think you are?" one of them shouted. Followed by, "You fucking wanker. I'll have you."

Jim gave a shrug of his shoulders.

"Outside, both of yous," he said in a quite calm voice.

The teddy boys said, "We'll beat the fuck out of you, you tosser."

Jim calmly walked out the door, followed by the two teddy boys.

"I've got to help him," Hazer said as he stood up. Raff followed him, but as they went to the door, Jim came back in with his forehead covered in blood.

"You alright?" Hazer asked.

"Noo worries", Jim said.

Raff and Hazer opened the door. There, lying on the floor, were the two teddy boys both unconscious.

"Fuck me," Raff said as he turned to Hazer.

Hazer smiled. He had another hero besides Boomer.

Jim stayed in Pompey, but after nine months he wanted to go home and the inevitable happened. He joined Jimmy Boile, a famous Glasgow gangster, got involved in a life of crime from bank robbery, extortion, armoured car heists. Hazer would visit Jim in Parkhurst Prison, Isle of Wight where he was involved in the riots and also at Dartmoor, where he was kept in solitary confinement for six months alongside Mad Frankie Fraser who was a London enforcer working for the Richardsons and Krays. He came back down to England between his prison holidays. He was always upbeat but his time in the nick was a waste of a young life, but he was a man of principle always.

So the Grove Club was off the boys' agenda and back to Hillside where Ernie and Peggy made them feel welcome.

"My God, look at the knockers on her," Plummy said. The boys turned round as this young lady entered Hillside, her bristols like two mountains preceding her body by at least a foot (that's big).

"I wouldn't mind getting my head in between them!" Plummy laughed.

The boys joined in "and me", "and me", "and me".

Then as she waddled past the boys, a voice from nowhere said "Giss a tit wobble" (meaning, let me put my penis between your knockers). The boys giggled, the young big-boobed lady turned to the gang, shook her head and carried on into the club, ignoring her admirers. The boys stood with their mouths open, a look of sheer lust on their dimly lit faces.

"I'll bet I'll have her," Austin announced.

"No chance," Raff replied. The rest of the gang nodded in

total agreement. She was too hot to touch.

The next day at school, the subject of the girl with mountains for breasts came up and one of the lads knew her brother so Austin had a name. Now he had to get in her good books.

"Sit," came the order. The boys made the usual sighs and scraping of chairs.

"This is your last term in my class. Most of you will be going straight to 4A, but a few of you will be going to 4B."

Hazer was confident he would be in the A stream, as was the rest of the gang except Micky Kimber. He had decided some time ago he didn't want to learn and he was true to his word, he didn't. So, in the new term, he was a C boy, dropped two classes and he didn't give a shit.

The Easter holidays

Camping, swimming, lazing about. This was what holidays were. Nobody went anywhere on an actual holiday.

"You coming up the hill?" Hazer asked the gang.

"Yeah," came the reply. Then a quiet girl's voice asked, "Can I come?" The gang smiled in unison. Hazer shrugged his shoulders.

"Do you reckon she can come?" he asked the rest of the hormone-raging teenagers.

"Well, suppose she can," Plummy said trying, not to sound keen.

The rest nodded in agreement, a couple tutting as if they were reluctant to take a young lady up the hill. The gang only reached halfway up the incline of Portsdown Hill when Plummy made out he'd hurt his ankle.

"Fuck me, I've twisted my ankle!" he screamed.

"Let me have a look," the young lady said as she bent over Plummy.

She began to unlace his winklepicker shoe, when he grabbed her. She fell on top of him.

"Giss a kiss," he said as he puckered his lips. To his surprise, she nearly swallowed him.

The boys stood wide eyed as Plummy wrestled on the green grass with this tigress.

"Come on, Plum, my turn," Austin said.

He rolled her over. "Show us your tits," he added.

Everybody was stunned when she undid her blouse and undid her bra, letting two ripe melons bounce in the summer air. Her nipples hard as two thimbles stood proud. Austin immediately dived on one, sucking it as if he was a newborn calf. Plummy wasn't going to miss out and dived for the other one, then bash. Plummy nutted Austin in a clash of heads.

"Fuck me, Plum," Austin shouted.

Plummy had forgotten his target and was holding his head, which was growing a walnut-sized bump. The young lady started to laugh. The gang joined in, but Austin was still attached to her left breast like a limpet sucking as if his life depended on it.

"Come on Mick, it's my turn," Raff said as he pulled Austin off.

"I was just getting her started," Austin complained.

As Raff started to strike one breast, a dog came from nowhere and joined him.

"Mick, that looks like your dog", Hazer said.

But he was too busy enjoying himself to take any notice.

"Mick, your mum and dad must be about," Hazer warned.

"Fuck off, Hazer," came the reply. Micky thought it was a spoof to get him to give up his enjoyment. Then on the ridge above the gang's heads, two shadowy figures appeared. The sun was directly behind them, their shadows cast onto the bottom of the dale, expanding as they reached the gang. Hazer put his hand over his eyes to shade the sun, then realised it was Mr and Mrs Rafferty out walking Bruce the dog, which was quite a regular occurrence.

Hazer shook Raff's shoulder. "Mick, it's your mum and dad," he whispered in Raff's ear.

"Fuck off, Hazer." Micky was having none of it.

"But Mick, honest…"

Then a trembling voice came from the shadow-throwing figures. "Michael, what are you doing?" Mrs Rafferty was clearly in a state of shock. Her Michael was an angel after all. In fact, all the gang's mums thought they were angels.

Raff looked up, his face turned a colour nobody had seen before or would see again throughout a lifetime.

"Get home now!" his dad roared.

The young lady didn't move, her tits still exposed to the disgruntled parents. The gang tried not to laugh, bowing their heads to the ground, waiting for the shadows to disappear over the horizon.

Micky Austin said, "My turn" as soon as Raff's parents left with Raff trailing behind them, his bowed head, turning around now and again to see Hazer and the lads waving bye bye in a somewhat sarcastic manner.

Under his breath, if they were nearer, the words 'You bastards' would have been heard. Raff was grounded for a week.

After he had left, "Giss a wank," Simmo asked.

"Fuck off, you'll get it on my dress." The young lady all of a sudden wasn't a young innocent girl.

So the boys had to promise not to get their mess on the young lady's attire.

They lined up in an orderly queue as she stroked each one off. So in the future, if she asked to join the gang of Portsdown Hill, they didn't hesitate to accommodate her.

Studying for exams

Hazer started to think about his future, what he wanted to do. He always fancied being in the Merchant Navy and seeing the world, a navigator, always sounded good to him. And the only way to get to his target was through the Portsmouth Dockyard Apprentice Scheme, which Mr Wells and Mr McCann highly recommended. But to take the entrance exam, Hazer would have to stay on at school till the summer. He could have left at Christmas and would have to prove to his teachers he was up to it. So along with several of his classmates, he stayed on at school after pleading with Jock to let him.

"You will noo do any good," Jock said in his Glaswegian accent.

"I'll really try, promise," Johnny pleaded.

"You'll be better off with me on the buildings."

"Let him try John." Audrey, Hazer's mum, always called Jock, John.

Jock shook his head. "Alreet, but he can work with the gangs on his Saturdays." Jock had given in.

So it was agreed Hazer would work with Ronnie August's gang on Saturdays.

At school, Hazer buckled down, no more clowning. He even volunteered for night school two days per week of extra lessons. 7 pm to 9 pm.

The first Saturday was a bit of a shock.

"Come on, get out that bed." Jock was shaking Hazer, who looked out the window to see nothing but darkness.

"What time is it?" he inquired, hoping it was a joke.

"Time to get out that bed the noo." Jock was growing

impatient with his only son and heir.

Johnny dragged himself out of his slumber, rolled out of bed, crawled out of his room to join Jock in the kitchen. He had a mug of sweet tea (four sugars) in one hand, a whiskey bottle in the other.

"You want a wee dram in your tea, son?" he asked his bleary-eyed, incoherent heir to his empire.

"No thanks, Jock," he answered, wondering how his dad could drink so early in the morning. It was 6.30 after all.

After a quick splash and cleaning his teeth, Johnny pulled on his old clothes.

"Here, you'd better put these on. It's a wee bit nippy out there," Jock said as he threw Johnny a set of dungarees.

Johnny got his legs in, pulled the rest over his shoulders. He sort of disappeared inside of this sack-like apparel. The dungarees were about four sizes too big so Johnny had to roll up both legs and arms about three turns.

"Put your wellies on. It's a wee bit muddy on the site," Jock added.

So Johnny shuffled to pull on his wellies over the turned-up dungarees.

"Come on then, hurry up or we'll be late," Jock called out as he downed the last drop of whiskey-laden tea.

Ronny August was waiting by Jock's car, alongside Boomer and a couple of other blokes who Johnny recognised.

"Morning Jock," Ronny said in a chirpy voice. He was always chirpy, as was his countenance. A round face, button nose, curly sandy coloured hair and a smile forever on his lips.

Hazer squeezed in the middle between Ronny and Jock. The car was a standard vanguard. Light blue in colour, with bench seats in the front and back with a column change gear stick

Jock started the engine, turned the heater on to the

windscreen to melt the early morning frost.

"I'll give it a scrape," Ronny said, so he went to the boot, removed the square-shaped trowel and attacked the windscreen till it was clear.

Jock lit up a fag, offering the packet to the men in the back. "Cheers Jock," one of them said.

"I'll open the window for you," Jock said as he knew Hazer hated the smoke.

So they were off. Johnny snuggled down trying to get warm. Soon he nodded off to the land of dreams.

"Come on John, we're here!" Ronny was shaking Hazer's shoulder. It was just beginning to get light. Johnny could make out half-built houses in the distance.

"Come on, we'll have a cuppa before we start."

A Romany-style caravan stood with its doors wide open. An old stove was belching out black smoke through its stove pipe in the roof, a large blackened kettle was emitting steam from on top of the stove. Johnny followed the others up the wooden steps. Inside were two benches either side of a long trestle table. Mugs were laid at one end.

A short tubby bloke had his back to them as they entered.

"This is Jock's boy, Jock," Ronny said.

"I'm not Jock," Hazer whispered.

Ronny laughed. "No, he's Jock" as the jovial-faced fellow turned to face them.

"Hello young man, how many sugars in your tea?" The new Jock spoke English. Johnny was puzzled. Why was he called Jock when he was English? Jock T was the tea boy; why he was called the tea boy, not the tea man was another great mystery to be solved and it was always in Hazer's head that Jock T made the tea.

"Two, please," Hazer answered.

Jock T preceded to pour the tea into a variety of mugs in

front of him. Everyone had their own mug, all different sizes and volumes.

"This will be your mug, young man." Jock handed Hazer a large enamelled mug with several chips in it, full to the top with steaming hot sweet tea.

"Thanks." Johnny didn't know what to call Jock.

"Jock," Jock said.

The rest of the men laughed.

Hazer cupped his hands around his tea mug. This not only warmed his cold hands, but gave him a feeling of being a welcomed member of the gang.

"Right, burn yee throats. There's work to be done," Jock said as he downed the last dregs of his whiskey-laden tea.

Instructions were given. "Mick and Bertie, finish that driveway. Boomer, you, Paddy and Jimmy complete that footing..."

"Son, you go with Ronny's gang."

"Come on, then," Ronnie smiled. So the dumper was started up after three or four turns of the starting handle.

"Remember when you start this, If the handle gets stuck, leave it and turn the engine off with this." Ronny pointed to a small lever on top of the engine as he was aware that the starting handle was prone to sticking.

A small shed was unlocked and the men grabbed various tools – shovels, forks, picks, trowels, wheelbarrows, etc.

"OK, let's go," Ronny said after loading the dumper with an assortment of tools.

"Jump on," he instructed Hazer, pointing to a flat piece of metal protecting the engine (no health and safety). Then they stopped next to a large cement mixer. It had a framework above it shaped like an inverted V. Two wires led from the top to a large shovel or scoop. On one of the handles were two buttons, red and green. The mixer was started up with the same type of handle as the dumper.

"Right, water in first." Ronny pointed to a large water butt, three buckets. "Then the cement." He lifted 100 weight bag as if it was a bag of sugar and threw it on the ballast and cut the cement bag in half with his shovel. He then chucked half in the mixer alongside the water, then pulling the shovel back, he scooped up a large amount of gravel and deposited it into the hungry mouth of the cement mixer, pushing the buttons on the handles till the mixer was half full, then the remaining cement went in plus another couple of buckets of water. Then the monster was fed with gravel till it was full.

"Got that?" Ronnie laughed.

Johnny watched in awe. "Yeah, I think so," he muttered.

Ronny drove the dumper to the other side of the mixer, turned the rotating barrel over and deposited the wet concrete snugly into the dumper's front bucket. The process then began again till the dumper was full. Johnny had tried to lift a bag of cement. He managed a couple of steps but nearly burst a blood vessel. So he was confined to the water bucket.

"You want to go on the scoop?" Ronny gave Hazer the instructions. "Make sure you take your finger off the green button when you're near the hopper."

Hazer was able to operate the scoop after several failed attempts. "Come on, get on," Ronny said, pointing to the makeshift seat.

Hazer sat on the dumper watching Ronny's every move, dipping the clutch when changing gear etc. Ronnie realised he was being scrutinised. "Want a go?" he shouted over the sound of the diesel-engined smoke-bellowing dumper.

"Can I?" Hazer shouted back.

"In a bit."

The concrete was delivered to the waiting, shuttered footpath, placed it was carefully tamped, a bevelled trowel was run along the edges and a flat trowel over the inside to be finished with a light brush to put lines across. This operation took some three visits to the mixer, i.e. three dumper loads.

Johnny was waiting for his chance to drive the dumper. At last, Ronnie said, "Come on, get in the driver's seat." He explained the workings. But Hazer wasn't listening properly as he was too excited, he thought it would be like the bumper cars at the fair at Easter. He took the gear stick, pressed the clutch, placed the stick forward, then let the clutch out as slowly as he could. Ronnie leaned over and released the handbrake. The dumper shot forward. Hazer bounced up. Ronnie nearly fell off, just grabbing the engine casing, which was hot as hell, burning his hand which he shook furiously. The dumper preceded to kangaroo through the muddy site. Hazer had a big smile on his face. He was a driver as his bum left the metal bucket-shaped seat with every kangaroo hop.

Ronny was wringing his hand, but looking at Hazer with a big grin on his face. He forgave him for not listening. So Hazer was a dumper driver. After a while, "Come on, it's tea up!" Jock T had blown a whistle in the distance. Back to the caravan, hot tea and bacon sandwiches were spread across the table.

"Get stuck in, young man," Jock T said.

Hazer took a large, doorstepped bacon sarnie. The butter was dripping through his fingers. "Thanks," he muttered, his mouth full of hot bacon, his mug of tea downed as quick as he could. He asked Ronny if he could practise on the dumper.

"OK, but be careful," he answered.

So Hazer preceded to circle the site on a lone exploration of his knew Saturday environment, bumping, kangarooing, a smile sometimes erupting on his face as he bounced, nearly leaving the seat behind him. Then back to work, more concrete had to be mixed and supplied till it was 1 pm. Jock emerged from his office, which was a wooden shed, about 10 foot by 15 foot in size with a large window and door on one side. The tools were put away. The men dusted themselves off as best they could before jumping back into Jock's car for the journey home or so Hazer thought.

After some ten minutes, the car took a sharp turn into a pub car park. The ritual had begun. Every pub on route back to Cosham was visited for a quick pint.

"Come on in," Jock said.

Hazer looked puzzled. He had only been allowed in the Bottle and Jug before. The Bottle and Jug was a small bar where you could buy beer to take away, plus crisps, lemonade, etc.

"Sit over there." Jock pointed to a table by the window.

Hazer sat down. Boomer joined him with two pint glasses of beer.

"Here, get this down yer," he said as he handed this 15-year-old his first brown split.

Johnny sipped his beer but didn't really like the taste, but he couldn't show his new work mates. The froth on the pint ended up on his nose. He tried to blow it off but ended up rubbing it off with his mud-bearing hand leaving a dark smudging on his face.

Back in the car, another two pubs, same ritual. Johnny's head was starting to spin and he wanted to pee for Britain. As the car turned into the George and Dragon in Cosham High Street he was on the verge of peeing his dungarees. He rushed into the outside toilets, his willy full of brown splits. He spent the next five minutes like a fireman, putting out a house blaze.

Jock said, "You coming in?" Hazer shook his head.

"Nah, I'm off home." He had drunk his quota. It was the first time he had been tipsy, despite Jock every new year forcing a dram down his throat to wish the world Hogmanay. Thanks Jock.

The next Saturday was much the same, but Hazer was the

dumper driver delivering concrete to all different gangs.

"I'm breaking my neck for a kase." Hazer questioned Bertie Shaw, a big man with dark hair, shiny cheeks, close lips, and two ears that nobody could see. "The thunder box is over there." He pointed to a small sentry-type box about 50 yards away.

"What, I got to have a dump in there?" Hazer said as if he was part of the gang.

"Yes, you got to have a crap in there," Bertie laughed.

Hazer was tossing up whether to shit his pants or go with the thunder box. The thunder box won. A small, solitary lonely piece of British architecture forgotten but as worthy as St Paul's Cathedral or York Minster, it stood alone awaiting Hazer's entrance like the police box in Doctor Who.

Hazer entered. The smell nearly knocked him off his tiny size 6 Frodo feet.

"Fucking hell" was heard around the site. He grimaced, but he had to have one. He did the business, then wiped his bum with last night's *Evening News*. Looking for a chain, Hazer realised there wasn't one, just a hole in the ground beneath the bowl, the turds still floating. Hazer's had joined them and was stuck to the mass. Hazer gulped, gulped again, ran out of the Tardis and was violently sick on the mud-stricken path. Jock T's bacon sarnies were sucked up into the mud as if it was alive.

"You alright?" Ronny inquired.

"Yeah, Ron," Hazer answered as the rest of the bacon sarnie left his mauve-coloured lips.

This ritual was carried out throughout his Saturdays. Hazer was part of a gang sitting in the gypsy caravan, sharing the sweet tea and bacon sarnies. He was part of a gang, but back at school he was determined to prove his team teachers wrong, so he buckled down and when it came to the dockyard entrance exams, he was as ready as anyone.

Rugby

It was tradition that at the end of the year in July before the break for the summer holidays, the teachers would play against the boys at either football or rugby. Hazer played for both teams, as did most of the football boys as rugby was just in house. The day arrived and it was rugby as the teachers knew the boys would hammer them at football. The boys were in the cloakroom, which doubled as a changing room. The teachers had changed in the main hall. Some struggled to fit into the kit, their bellies protruding like an unwanted pregnancy above their black shorts. The school was watching from the sidelines as the teams entered the arena that was the top field. The teachers came first, talking amongst themselves, each one wishing this tradition was abandoned in the next five minutes and they could go home and enjoy six weeks of freedom. The boys entered to cheers worthy of Roman gladiators.

Hazer turned to Upsall, laughed, and then tripped over his boot laces, which he had not tied properly. The school was watching as he fell face first into the rain-soaked ground. Upsall picked him up. The mud was still attached to Hazer's now non-grinning face. Hazer's face was a bright red, but thanks to the mud, the pupils of Portsdown Academy for Young Gentlemen hadn't a clue.

The game commenced. The boys were a lot faster than their educational betters. But the ref was an – you guessed it – educational better, Mr Evans. Every time the boys entered the brains' half, the whistle went for some misdemeanour or other.

The teachers, led by Mr Cook and Mr Cooper, who were the PE instructors, ran riot with complete immunity from the referee. The boys were completely fucked. The scores at half time (not that anyone in Hazer's team bothered, the teachers always won, no matter what) was 22–0.

The whistle blew for half time. The ex-football now rugby team sat down on the damp grass. The teachers huddled round. Somebody produced a small silver flask which they each took a sip out of.

The second half commenced much the same as the first, until a scrum down was awarded. Hazer threw the ball into the mass of the scrum, went to the rear of his team to receive the ball which was worked back to him. He clutched the ball and started to run like hell. To his surprise, nobody chased him. He dived over the line. Placing the ball down for a try, he rose up to see the teachers and his teammates with puzzled faces. Then he realised. He had ran the wrong way and had scored a try for the teachers. "Well done, Hayes," Mr Cook said, a dirty grin on his face. So Hazer's only try in rugby was a monumental cock-up.

The end of school days

It was into 4A for Hazer and most of his mates. Football season started straight away, but after another altercation with another schoolteacher, Hazer, Raff and Upsall were not allowed to play. But they were now playing regularly for Hillside Youth Club in the Portsmouth Lads League. This was a much higher grade than school football and it meant they were playing alongside boys two years older than them. And against much more experienced opponents. Ernie Littlefield and Charlie Coles ran the teams from Hillside.

The boys played on a Saturday afternoon so watching Pompey was a no go unless a game was called off due to the weather conditions.

The boys were playing at Farlington Marshes one Saturday afternoon. Ernie was manager the team were getting changed into the kit when two older blokes entered the changing room.

Ernie said, "What you want?"

"Just came to say good luck," one of them murmured.

"Well fucking say it and get out," Ernie glared.

"Good luck, boys," the other bloke said.

"Who was that?" Hazer asked Dave Jackson.

"They run the Lads League," he answered.

"Ernie don't like 'em much, does he?" Hazer questioned.

Ernie heard Hazer's remarks

"Boys, before you go out, the two blokes who just left are a couple of shirtlifters, so watch yourselves, alright? You have been warned."

The team nodded to each other. "They try it on us, we'll beat the crap out of them," somebody said. The rest of the team gave a snarl in agreement. The two gentlemen who represented the Lads League kept away from Hillside Boys for most of the season but back at Farlington on the second to last game of the year, Hillside had to win to confirm winning the league. They duly won 3–0 with goals from Raff, Cummings and Upsall.

Ernie wasn't there, so Charlie Coles was manager for the day. The boys noticed the shirtlifters watching the game. The half-time whistle had gone when the plan was hatched between the team as they munched on half an orange each to give them energy for the next 45 minutes.

The game over, the boys retired to the changing rooms ready for a shower. Charlie was collecting the shirts as the two shirtlifters entered the room. "Well done, boys," one said.

The team looked at each other, then in unison turned with their backs to the two, dropped their shorts, bent over showing their white arses, then shouted, "Up yours, you fucking poofs, piss off."

The aftermath: Every year a team was sent from Portsmouth Lads League to play a team in Duisburg, Germany. A free holiday for the boys who were picked, but despite winning the leagues and winning or being runners-up in the cups, nobody from that Hillside team was considered to represent the Lads League. Those two did indeed abuse young boys and got away with it.

To take the dockyard entrance exam, Hazer, along with Austin and Simmo, had to stay on at school for an extra two terms. Raff, Polly and several other boys left at Christmas to go out into the big wide world.

Jock had taken his son and heir to have a suit made by a proper tailor, not off the peg.

Every year, Jock and his mates would go to Goodwood

horse races. Jock decided it was time for Hazer to join them, hence the suit.

Jock had bought a new car, a Vauxhall Cresta. Hazer, who had continued to go to work on Saturday mornings, had, with Jock's, permission driven his new car around the estate roads, learning as he went, changing gears, reversing, etc. After all, he was 15 years old. He was getting used to driving around the site roads. The only thing was he needed was a cushion to sit on so he could see out the windscreen.

The races

Jock was up early waking Hazer with a cuppa. Hazer got up and joined Jock in the kitchen where he was busy murdering breakfast, cigarette dangling from the side of his mouth. A wee dram was poured into his tea before he took a sip.

"Goodwood today, son," he smiled.

"Yeah, I know." Hazer would rather be with his mates, although he liked gambling on the horses. A tanner each way on a horse now and then with Mr Rolf who was a bookies runner as there were no betting shops and gambling off track was illegal. Ronny Rolf had introduced Hazer to betting on the gee-gees.

Jock dished up the breakfast crispy bacon, that when you tried to cut it splintered all over the plate. Hard yoked fried eggs, black pudding (care of Scotland) and beans burnt so they stuck to the pan.

"Get that doon ya, son. It's goo'n a be a long day," Jock said as he crunched his teeth onto the splintered bacon, supping his whiskey tea to soften the pain.

Johnny got ready, a brand-new shirt, and tie accompanied his dog-toothed suit, a purple pair of socks was pulled onto each foot. Then his Chukka boots were tied with a double bow.

A knock on the door, and Boomer and Ronny August joined them in the kitchen.

"Morning Boom," he said.

"Want a wee drink, boys?" Jock said.

"Don't mind if I do." Ronny added, "Got any beer?"

Jock pointed to a crate of brown ales, courtesy of

Brickwoods. "Help yourselves," he said. Ronny bent down picked two bottles up, threw one to Boomer. They unscrewed the stoppers and began to savour the taste of Brickwoods' finest ale. A knock on the door, and they were joined by Kenny Wearn. (Jock and Aud's knew neighbours Kenny and Pammy had a multitude of children and as the years went on, Jock and Kenny became very close friends.)

Ronny revisited the crate again and handed Kenny a beer.

"Right, you's ready?" Jock said, rising from his chair.

So the smartly dressed gentlemen headed for Jock's new car. Ronny was carrying the crate of beer which he placed in the boot, after taking another four bottles out for the journey.

They headed towards Chichester. After 20 minutes, Jock pulled into a pub car park. It was 11 am. "We'll have a wee drink and visit the loo," he said as he pulled the handbrake on.

Twenty minutes later, they re-embarked in the Vauxhall Cresta only to stop in another three pubs before entering the car park at Goodwood Racecourse.

Johnny was gobsmacked; he had never seen such a place. The grandstand was overlooking the magnificent South Downs. You could see for miles. Portsmouth and the Isle of Wight spread out like a carpet of colour, to the southwest and Littlehampton and onto Brighton to the southeast, and the hills and dales of the South Downs to the north.

The racecourse ran in a large arc in front of them. The grass was green as any Hazer had seen.

"You want a shandy?" Boomer asked Hazer as he leaned on the bar, a crisp pound note waving in his hands to attract the barman.

"I'll have a coke, Boom," Hazer replied, adding "no straw."

Hazer clutched his coke and left the gang chatting away, swigging back the pints of ale and studying the form in the racing papers.

Hazer went to explore this grand edifice. Turning the corner, he spotted the saddling arena. He headed there. What he saw took his breath. The horses were nothing like he had ever seen, lean, beautiful-coated stallions and mares were being saddled by their grooms. The only horses Hazer had seen were pulling carts around the streets of Pompey. These were superb animals. Hazer fell in love with these atmospheric surroundings.

He turned and followed the saddled horses to the parade ring. The colours of the jockeys' shirts glistened in the sun. Hazer had only seen racing on a black-and-white television, and that was the Grand National once a year, but this was something else. The jockeys were in deep conversation with the trainers and owners, now and again hitting their riding boots with the whips they were carrying.

A bell rang out and the jockeys started to mount up. They proceeded to circle the parade ring. Hazer was leaning against the rail as these fabulous animals and their rainbow-coloured riders passed. He could almost reach out and touch them.

"You enjoying yourself?" a voice came from behind. Hazer felt a hand on his shoulder.

"Yeah," Hazer answered as he turned to face Kenny Wearn.

With that, Kenny proceeded to point out the jockeys and the names of the horses.

"That's Lester Piggott. That's Scobie Breasley."

"I bought you another coke," he said as he handed it to Hazer.

"Thanks mate," Jonny acknowledged Kenny.

The horses left the ring; Hazer followed as they entered the racecourse proper. The sound of the hooves sent a chill down his back as they galloped past him. Kenny asked him if he was alright as he turned to join the gang in the beer tent.

"Yeah," Hazer answered.

Hazer walked towards a throng of people standing looking up at numerous boards accompanied by men shouting out the odds of the horses. Then he noticed a couple of men standing on large crates waving their white-gloved hands like lunatics. He gave a puzzled look, wondering what they were doing. Released out of the loony bin or were they Al Johnson impersonators? Then he was joined by the beer-breathed gang, each holding pound notes in their hardworn mitts. Jock went up to a bookmaker, pointed to the board and handed him ten crisp notes. The bookie shouted to his mate. He was bent over a large book. Then he gave Jock a small ticket. The rest of the gang followed suit, only with one or two crisp notes. Jock then turned to Hazer, shouted the name of the horse he had backed. Hazer nodded to acknowledge that he had got the name. He looked at the board till he located Jock's horse's number. Number 3. Lester Piggott was the jockey.

The loudspeaker roared into action. "They're under orders!" and a few seconds later "and they're off!"

Hazer was on the rail about 100 yards from the winning post. He leant over as far as he could to see the horses galloping towards him and their goal, the winning post. It seemed an age, then above the crowd's noise the thunder of hooves filled his ears again as they came closer and closer. Then, like a flash of lightning, they stormed past him. If he had blinked, he would have missed them. Bloody hell, Jock's horse was in the lead with 100 yards to go. Johnny couldn't wait to join his dad and tell him the good news. Then the tannoy sang out again. Photo finish. Hazer's heart sank, he crossed his fingers for good luck. After waiting five minutes the tannoy crackled into life.

"The winner is number…"

Hazer crossed all his fingers on both hands and closed his

eyes, wishing the number three would follow.

"Number 7!" was announced.

Hazer witnessed hundreds of people tearing up their tickets and the lucky few queuing at the bookmakers' desks to be paid out.

Kenny located Hazer at the rail with another coke. "Who's the looney waving his arms about, Ken?" he inquired.

"Oh, that's the tic tac man," Kenny answered.

"What's a tic tac man?" Hazer was more puzzled than ever.

Kenny pointed across the stadium to another group of bookmakers about 75 yards away. They had their own lunatics waving their white-gloved hands.

Kenny went on to explain that they were sending messages to each other via hand signals and the gloves weren't meant to imitate Al Johnson as Hazer had conjured up in his mind, but so the signals could be easily seen. He went on to explain about the odds and if somebody in the know placed a bet, the odds would come down.

The day continued until the sun started to fade as it moved westward across the clear blue sky towards Pompey.

Hazer joined the gang in the beer tent after the last race. The merry gang were downing the last dregs of ale. Jock was smiling in a drunken sort of way, Boomer and Ronny were leaning with their backs to the bar, swirling their glasses as if to say goodbye to an old friend before swallowing.

"Time, gentlemen, please." It was over. Hazer's first day at the races, one he would remember forever in a happy, nostalgic way.

Dockyard exam

It was Hazer's last term at school. Raff and a few others had left to enter the working world. Hazer, Austin and Simmo had stayed to take the dockyard apprenticeship exams.

Hazer had this idea. He wanted to see the world, and according to Mr Wells, the best way was to serve an apprenticeship then join the Merchant Navy as a junior officer. So this was Hazer's plan. He got his head down at school and studied till his head was full. The day of exams came. It was to take place at the Dockyard College at Flathouse Quay in Stamshaw.

Micky, Hazer and Simmo boarded the bus at the top of Cosham, after meeting in Milly's cafe.

"You nervous?" Simmo asked his two mates as they boarded the bus and went upstairs.

"Nah," Austin shrugged.

Hazer kept quiet but inside his stomach the butterflies were fluttering their wings as they had done before every boxing match he had taken part in.

Austin and Simmo lit up a fag, each trying to blow smoke rings but failing miserably.

Hazer still wouldn't try a fag even though his mates tried to pressure him into joining them.

They alighted the bus opposite the gates to Flathouse Quay. It was a hive of activity behind the walls, the apprentices in their brown dungarees, hurrying and scurrying in and out of the multitude of brick-built buildings.

A Navy policeman stood at the gate. A queue of young teenagers were waiting. They joined the queue as it snaked towards him.

Hazer's turn came.

"Name?" the policeman asked.

"Hayes," came the reply.

"First name."

"John Hayes."

The officer consulted his list which was clipped to a board.

"OK, Mr Hayes, follow the other lads," he said as he ticked off Hazer's name.

Johnny waited for Simmo and Austin. The butterflies seemed to be exploding in his stomach. They entered a large hall. Rows of desks stood, each accompanied by a single chair, a gap of about a yard between each aisle.

"Take a seat," ordered a rotund gentleman dressed in tweeds.

The room must have held a total of 80 or so desks. Each aisle was patrolled by a tutor to eliminate any chance of cheating. Hazer took his place, a booklet stamped with 'dockyard entrance exam' looked up at him from the desk. The sharpened pencil was in its slot with a pencil sharpener placed beside it. The rotund gentleman spoke.

"Settle down. You have two hours to complete this exam. No talking will be allowed. Anyone caught cheating will be dismissed. Understood?"

The boys looked around, some nodded, others just grunted in agreement.

Hazer opened the paper and quickly devoured page after page. The butterflies were gone. He tore into the exam paper and after an hour and a half he was finished. He looked up and noticed one or two of the lads had also completed the paper. He sat for a while, then a tutor whispered in his ear, "Spend the next half hour going over your paper, checking your answers." Wise words indeed, because Hazer did find a couple of his calculations to be incorrect.

"OK times up. Put your names and school on the paper, then hand them to me. Thank you, gentlemen."

As they met outside, Austin and Simmo had lit up and were still trying to blow smoke rings in vain.

"How do you get on?" Hazer inquired.

Simmo grunted, "Dunno, alright I suppose."

"What about you, Mick?"

Austin shrugged his shoulders and continued to puff away on his fag.

About two weeks later, a letter arrived from the dockyard. Hazer had to go for an interview, accompanied by one of his parents or a guardian.

The day soon arrived for the interview. Jock had made his son and heir put on his new suit and tie. Jock, also dressed in his best suit, was ready to be questioned about his eldest and only boy.

"Come in, Mr Hayes," the portly gentleman requested as he poked his head around the half-open door. "Don't forget your son," a wry remark that he had made on numerous occasions.

So Hazer and Jock entered the room to be confronted by five middle-aged gentlemen.

"Take a seat, please." The man in the middle gestured to the two empty chairs in front of the long desk at which they were seated.

"Let me introduce myself and my colleagues," he said, going through their names which by the end Hazer and Jock had forgotten.

The questions came thick and fast. Why did you want an apprenticeship? Hobbies, etc. Hazer answered enthusiastically. When it came to Jock's questions they were completely flummoxed as each inquiry asked of Jock was met with a broad Glaswegian accent that they couldn't understand. So a nod and "Yes, I see" were the only replies they could give to Jock's garbled Scots talk.

A few weeks later, the letter arrived. Hazer had excelled himself, coming eighth out of 400 boys who had sat the exam. So he had the pick of apprenticeships along with the top 30 boys. He chose to study electrical engineering. Austin – fitter and turner – and Simmo – shipwright. So into the wide world, they would go at the end of term.

The school dance

Mr Cook, who had not been very unfriendly with Hazer, seemed to change when Hazer started to behave (i.e. he knew his job), so Hazer settled down, studied and behaved himself.

"We are arranging a school dance," Mr Cook announced at school, slowly adding "for the 4th and 5th year leavers. It will be held in the Senior Girls school. If it's a success, this could become an annual event."

Then he read a list of boys' names who would help organise the dance. To Hazer's surprise, he was on the list

"The boys I've named, meet me in the gym after school. That's if you want to be involved."

Hazer turn to Faithfull and Upsall who also were named. "What you think?" he asked.

Simmo butted in. "I'll go if you don't want to."

"Nah, suppose we'll have to go. All those girls must be fighting over us," Upsall laughed as he showed his muscled arms.

"OK. Glad you all turned up," Mr Cook said.

"Wouldn't miss it for the world, sir," came a cocky-voiced Hazer.

Mr Cook grinned. "Tomorrow morning, meet here after roll call. I've sorted it with your teachers."

So next morning the seven privileged sex-mad teenagers were let loose in the gym of Portsdown Senior Girls school.

Mr Cook and two lady teachers were organising the decorations. As the boys carried out their instructions, hanging various ex-Christmas gear about the stage, a whistle blew and the door to the gym opened. A class of girls dressed in white shirts and skimpy skirts entered the hall.

"Don't mind us," one of the lady teachers informed the gym teacher.

"OK girls, stop the giggling," Mrs Gym Teacher roared.

So the girls started to perform their exercises, bending, twisting, jumping, each one aware of the seven teenage sex-mad boys trying to hang decorations on the stage.

"Cool, look at them jumping up and down," Simmo nudged Hazer.

Hazer took a glance. It was big boobs from Hillside.

"Please keep your mind on your work," Mr Cook whispered in Simmo's ear. Simmo somehow had wrangled his way onto the squad. The boys continued to hang the decor, but the occasional glance couldn't be helped, especially when big boobs got near to the stage. Hazer was holding onto the stepladder whilst Faithfull was at the top when Hazer's attention was drawn by Upsall – the girls were doing press-ups, their bums facing the stage. Upsall nudged Hazer. "What would you do with that?" he mimed. Hazer turned too quickly. The rickety stepladder started to move. "Fuck me!" rang out around the hall as Faithfull came to join the other boys on the stage, with a loud thwack.

The girls doing press-ups all turned their heads on hearing Faithfull swearing and tumbling off the ladder. Some couldn't help bursting out in laughter. Faithfull jumped up, dusted himself down, his face turned a purple colour.

"You alright, mate?" Upsall asked, trying not to join the girls in laughter.

"Yeah," came the reply.

Hazer said sorry and made an excuse. It was the rickety stepladder, not him being distracted by the sight of 30 or so girls, bums going up and down in unison as if doing the act.

Mr Cook and the two lady teachers heard the profanity, but

as Faithfull had taken a fall, nothing was carried any further.

"OK, now Mr Best, you're in the electronics class."

"Yes, sir."

"And you, Mr Stamp [Podsey]."

"Yes, sir."

"We have to wire up the speakers to the record player. And as you are familiar with electrics…" he stopped mid-sentence and pointed to the equipment.

"OK, sir," Podsey said.

So Bestie and Podsey set to work, arranging wires and speakers about the stage, all rigged to a microphone in front of the record player.

"How's it going?" Mr Cook inquired.

"Nearly there, sir," Podsey said.

"All done. Switch it on," instructed Bestie.

A switch was thrown. Hazer and the rest were expecting an explosion but nothing happened. Just a crackling noise coming from the microphone

"OK, sir, if you want to play a record."

Mr Cook and the lady teachers chose a record from the stack next to the Dansette, placed the needle and waited for the music to play. The girls had stopped performing and were watching, waiting for pop music to burst out like they had at Hillside. But it was Vera Lynn that surrounded them in the hall.

"Perfect, well done boys," one of the lady teachers said.

So that night, Portsdown's girls and Portsdown's boys met on the first school dance ever held, but it wasn't Vera Lynn. It was Chubby Checker and the twist that blared out around this hall, with a hundred or so teenagers twisting the night away, as Chubby Checker would sing.

Leaving school

Mr Pearson was a hippy before hippies were known. Long straggly hair, denim jeans, a cravat around his neck, a small goatee beard hung from his chin, always a smile on his face. He took Hazer's class for the last term of his school years.

Roll call was casual. No. Yes Sir, no Sir. It was like being a grown-up with Mr Pearson. He introduced Hazer to George Orwell, HG Wells and other writers whose works Hazer had never heard of. So when it was Mr Pearson's English lesson, no writing, just reading whatever book you liked. Then maybe a discussion on whatever subject came up from the reading.

Mr Pearson was an avid reader, joining the class as they read, but one day the book he was reading was not left on his desk as usual, but locked in his drawer during break. This intrigued Austin and Hazer. So they decided to corner Mr Pearson.

"OK boys, what did you think of *Animal Farm*?" Mr Pearson asked.

A couple of lads grunted, imitating the pigs in animal farm. A couple said it's alright. Those are the ones who hadn't bothered to read it and had just whiled away the lesson looking out the windows.

"Really enjoyed it, sir," Austin said." But what you reading?" he added.

"Yes, sir," Hazer joined in. "What are you reading?"

Mr Pearson was stuck for an answer.

"It's a bit too adult for you." His face was starting to redden.

"But sir, you always tell us we are young adults."

"Come on, sir," someone else called out.

"Yes!" the class joined in, seeing Mr Pearson's face.

"It's called *Lady Chatterley's Lover*," he gave in.

"Sir, I have seen that on the telly it's banned." Austin's question was right on the bullseye.

"What you doing with a banned book, sir?" someone said.

"It's not banned," Mr Pearson answered.

"Can we read it then, sir?" Hazer had him.

"No you can't."

"Why not, sir, you said we were adults," another class member had added his two penneth.

"What's it about then, sir?"

Mr Pearson sank back into his chair, trying to find an excuse not to reveal the reason the boys couldn't read *Lady Chatterley's Lover*.

"It's a love story, so you wouldn't like it."

Someone at the back of class shouted, "Do they do it, sir?"

"Yeah!" added another.

"Do what?" Mr Pearson had heard the remark.

"You know, sir, shagging and that." Upsall always came straight to the point.

"I think that's enough on that subject." Mr Pearson closed his book and placed it back in the drawer. Some days later, Mr Pearson was called away, leaving his desk drawer unlocked. This was the opportunity they had been waiting for.

"Keep watch," Austin said.

So Hazer opened the door leading to the corridor, poked his head round. "All clear," he said.

Austin extracted the 'Lady Chat' book. He noticed some pages were marked, so he opened the book at these pages and started to read out loud the reason some people wanted to ban this book.

The class were in hysterics. Hazer could hear everything. Then Mr Pearson appeared at the end of the corridor.

"Quick, he's coming back!" he shouted to Austin, who replaced the book and re-joined the class at his desk.

Mr Pearson entered the room. "Now where was I before the interruption?" he said.

Some bright spark sitting at the back of class shouted out, "Giving Lady Chatterley one in the potting shed." Mr Pearson shook his head as he realised he had left the drawer unlocked.

The class started to laugh. A smile broke from Mr Pearson. "OK, I know, can we now get down to work?"

The last days of school seemed to drag on. All the leavers were given a Gideons Bible (New Testament) which they took to each teacher to sign and say their goodbyes. Hazer got a bit choked up knowing he wouldn't be a pupil of Portsdown Academy For Young Gentleman, but a dockie alongside thousands of other dockies in the big wide world of industry.

Mr Wells, Mr Palmer, Mr Evans, Mr McCann, Mr Jones, Mr Bucket, Mr Cook, and all the other teachers had over the years in the senior school changed Hazer's attitude from the hot-headed lunatic to something resembling a normal schoolboy and on his last day all the good and not so good times flashed through Hazer's mind, and he found himself quietly reflecting on the last five years. A small tear started to roll down his cheek.

"You alright, Hayes?" Mr Wells asked as he shook his hand.

"Yes, sir."

"OK, run along. There's a big wide world out there."

Hazer turned and left Mr Wells standing at the school gates. He never went back to that outstanding school, but the memories would be with him till his days were spent.

Thank you to all the wonderful teachers and staff of Portsdown Infants, Junior and Senior boys schools.

Conway Street

Hazer's first day at work. He was given a card showing how to clock in, then shown to his workspace, a large thick oak table with a vice attached, several files and rasps were in a cradle. The instructor introduced himself and preceded to explain the first task which was to file a piece of brass to a certain size, which would be measured with a micrometre to so many thousands of an inch.

Hazer couldn't see the point. He was, after all, an electrical engineer. After a morning of filing, he was as bored as shit, so were 90% of his fellow inmates. This was supposed to instil patience and discipline into the apprentices, but after a few days of filing the boys were going up the wall.

The next week was payday. Friday morning, the whole unit lined up in classes to receive their wages in a brown envelope which had a small window in it. Hazer opened his first wage packet. It held two pounds and 19 shillings and 10 pennies. He had to give his mother a pound for his keep, so he had for a week of filing a lump of brass, two pounds, all but tuppence to himself.

After a few weeks, different exercises were introduced. Two days a week was spent at the College in Flathouse Quay, learning about basic electrics. Hazer was bored to death. Being indoors didn't suit him, but he had made some great new friends who decided they wanted to form a band. Some could actually play the guitar. They needed a singer, so Hazer, who was always singing Elvis songs, was persuaded to become part of the band. They proceeded to make their own amplifiers out of stolen valves etc. from Conway Street.

Hazer had bought a second-hand electric guitar for 30 bob, but no matter how he tried, he couldn't sing and coordinate his hands, so all the other band members told him to make it look like he was playing, but his kit was switched off.

They practised in the upstairs room in a pub. The noise was horrific. They went to as many package shows as possible. Package shows work where several artists performed down the Guildhall, Portsmouth. The occasional visit to the Gaumont Theatre in Southampton to see the great American artists like Chuck Berry, Little Richard, Jerry Lee Lewis was also on the agenda. These were the songs, plus a few Elvis renditions, they practised above the pub. The noise level was like an express train at full speed.

After several weeks, they thought they were ready, so downstairs in the public bar was their first gig. It was shit!

Hazer, who had gone to Brighton one weekend, had watched a band called The Who. The lead singer would twirl the microphone around, swinging it between his legs and above his head. Hazer hadn't told the band he was going to try the same manoeuvre. So when it came to 'Johnny Be Good', Chuck Berry, he tried his luck. The back feed was horrendous. The static nearly deafened the pub dart team who were about to start a match.

He was Roger Daltrey of The Who until he swung the mic around his head once too often and one of the darts team carrying two pints of beer, received a microphone around the back of his head, causing him to spill the ale all over the pub floor. Hazer's face turned yellow.

"Fuck me, Hazer," one of the band shouted. Hazer gulped and mouthed "Sorry!" to the recipient of his over-exuberant use of the mic. The landlady had witnessed this little episode and decided to literally pull the plug, which brought a welcome silence to the public bar and an end to Hayes's antics and his showbiz life. He continued to practise the guitar but never mastered it.

It was driving his sister Jeannie mad. The noise was like a screaming hedgehog mating. One day, Hazer's door was flung open. In the doorway, was his little sister holding a pint glass of water.

"What's up, Jean?" he questioned.

"Your fucking music!" she shouted as she threw the water over Hazer and his makeshift amplifier.

A loud bang, the sparks lit the room. Hazer had just let go of his electric guitar or he would have been fried toast.

"Fuck me, Jean!" he shouted.

"Serves you right!" she shouted back.

The amp was kaput. So were Hazer's dreams of rock stardom. But he forgave his sister.

Happy as a sandboy

"What is a sandboy?" he asked his nan.

She shrugged her apron-clad shoulders as she continued to stir the washing in the boiler, the cigarette dangling from her bottom lip had long gone out.

"Silly boy! How should I know? Ask Granddad."

"Never mind, I was just wondering," he replied.

Hazer was always wondering, thinking why this, why that. The year before, his mum had caught him with a big smile on his face and had said you look as happy as a sandboy. Hazer couldn't tell his mum what had happened the previous night.

"What you do'in tonight? Miss A asked Hazer.

"Don't know, why?" he asked.

"I'm babysitting for my sister."

"So what?"

"You want to help?"

"What, baby sit? No thanks." He shrugged his shoulders.

With that, Miss A reached out and touched him in a very private place. His face lit up! A smile like a sandboy covered his nearly unfreckled face.

"You mean?" he gave thrust with his hips.

"If you're nice to me." A wicked grin erupted on her lips.

"What time?"

"About eight."

"I'm supposed to be going down the club with my mates."

She gave another wicked grin, as she whispered, "I'll let you have me!"

"Fuck the club," Hazer thought. He couldn't wait for that evening to come. He made a special point of washing every bit of his body twice over. He spent 20 minutes on his teeth and hair. He looked in the mirror, checked how cool he looked, gave himself a nod. "You're ready," he mouthed softly.

The gang were waiting at the meeting point as usual at 7.30 pm, ready to saunter to Hillside.

Hazer had to make an excuse and not join them on their journey to the rock 'n' roll factory that was Hillside on a Friday night.

Raff, Teddy, Roffey, Corrigan and a couple of others were already at the bars, ready for the off, each one hoping to get lucky with one of the beehive-haired girls awaiting them over the club. (Girls had their hair shaped like a beehive which was held in place by copious amounts of lacquer.)

Hazer joined the gang just as they were leaving. "Come on, Hazer," Teddy gestured with his arm.

"Shit," he said. "I'll catch you up."

"What's up?" Teddy asked.

"Forgot my money. Left it on the side." Hazer tried to sound convincing, emptying his pockets as he did so.

He turned and walked back towards his house. "We'll wait," somebody said. "No, I'll catch you up," Hazer insisted.

So the group left the bars outside Kenny Hill's paper shop and headed for Hillside, laughing and joking as they went. Hazer ducked into Mrs Shaw's alley, waited ten minutes, then emerged, ready for his first sortie into the unknown.

He crept down the garden path and up to the front door of the ground floor flat, hoping he hadn't been spotted by the neighbours. He gently pulled the door knocker back and tapped it three times, nothing stirred. He tried again only a bit louder. The curtain moved. A smiling face appeared at the window. She mouthed, "I won't be a minute" then disappeared again.

Hazer waited, then after two minutes the door opened. Miss A stood there holding a young infant in her arms, the dummy was stuck between the baby's lips and a saggy nappy was hanging halfway down the toddler's bum.

"Come in," Miss A beckoned with her non-baby-holding hand. Hazer closed the door behind him and joined Miss A in the sparsely furnished front room. The Sound of Music was coming from the radiogram in the corner.

"You alright?" Miss A asked.

"Yes, suppose so."

"Don't worry, the baby will be asleep in no time."

Hazer nodded, thinking to himself "I bloody hope so."

He sat on the sofa trying not to look bored.

As Miss A rocked the baby in her arms, humming a lullaby, after half an hour the baby was still very much awake and every time it was introduced to its cot it started to holler. Hazer was getting pissed off but he couldn't show it, so he sat there and suffered, wishing he had joined his mates down the club.

Time was getting on. The small mantle clock was showing 9.30. Hazer knew the pubs shut at 10:30 so time was running out fast.

"There, there, there, there," Miss A said softly as at last the baby's eyes closed. She gently laid the baby in his cot, turned to Hazer and smiled.

"Come on then," she said, leading Hazer to the bedroom. Hazer could feel his heart beating. "This is it," he thought as he pushed open the bedroom door. She beckoned him with her little finger.

"Come here," she whispered. As she lowered her knickers to the floor, Hazer nearly came in his pants, which were new ones (nobody ever had pants in this era). He could not help himself. He leapt onto Miss A. His dick was like the Blackpool Tower, with its lights crossing the Irish Sea. She took him in her arms, caressed his aching body, and took him to a world he had never experienced.

No. What really happened was Hazer entered the bedroom, Miss A lay on the bed, legs akimbo. Hazer was so excited he didn't know if he had done it or just shaved her thighs. That's what happens when you're young.

"You alright, John," she asked. Hazer sat there, hoping the baby would wake up and rescue him.

"Yes," he answered.

"Do you want to have a cuddle?" Miss A asked.

Hazer was in limbo. He had done it, but he didn't feel anything for the girl he had just done it with. It was like being in a love affair when only one person was in love. All the time, he felt the guilt, but his lower regions ruled his teenage years.

Hazer couldn't face Miss A as all he wanted to do was to get out of there.

Miss A realised she had been used so tried to put a brave face on. "Do you want a cup of tea?" she asked as she wrestled with her knickers.

Hazer shook his head. Now he was as embarrassed as Miss A.

"I'll make sure the baby's alright," Miss A whispered.

"Yeah, I hope we didn't make wake him," Hazer answered.

Miss A disappeared into the baby's room.

Hazer was trying to think up ways to get out of there. Miss A re-entered the room carrying the baby.

"You want to hold him?" she asked.

Hazer nearly shit himself. "Fuck me, she wants a baby. I gotta get out of here." His mind was racing. Panic was setting in. Then to his relief the garden gate was slammed.

"Must be your sister. I better be going," he said, as he pulled his jacket on.

"You can stay if you want. She won't mind."

Hazer's face screwed up. "Nah, better be going."

So as he opened the front door, Miss A's big sister and her husband stood there, his face was bright red as he lowered his brow.

"Hello sis," Miss A's voice echoed behind him. "Johnny was keeping me company."

Hazer was saved.

"You want a cuppa?" Big Sis asked.

"Nah, got to be up early in the morning."

Hazer made his excuse, pushed past the couple and vanished into the night.

The first game of the season was coming up. The Hillside team was ready after three friendly games. This was their final year in the Lads League.

Hillside football teams were unbeatable from the Men's Premier League to junior leagues and Lads league.

The first game was at Farlington rec. Some 20 minutes in and Hazer got a nasty kick in his kneecap. His knee swelled up like a balloon as he lay on the floor. Ernie sauntered over, a fag in his mouth, with a bucket and sponge to administer first aid.

"Let's have a look," he said as he examined Hazer's torn kneecap. "Just a scratch," he added.

"Fuck me, Ern, it's fucking killing me," Hazer growled.

"You'll be alright. Play out on the wing." He gestured to the winger Bobby Gadson. "You play in the middle. Hazer can go one on the wing." There were no substitutes in those days.

So Hazer struggled on the wing for the rest of the game, damaging his knee even more. After the game, Hazer hobbled home helped by his teammates. His knee was swollen so much he couldn't pull up his drainpipe jeans, so he had to wrap a towel around his waist, hobble to the bus stop, and make his way home.

"Let's have a wee look," Jock said as he inspected Hazer's

knee. "We'll leave it till the morning. See if the swelling goes doon."

Hazer nodded, hoping Jock was right and it wasn't as bad as it felt.

Hazer was in agony all night, so Jock decided it was worth a hospital visit.

Hazer hadn't had any type of injury whilst playing footy or boxing or climbing trees, so he hadn't been to hospital, only as a visitor. It was the Royal in Commercial Road, Portsmouth, where accident and emergencies were taken. Jock helped Hazer out of the car, placed him in a wheelchair, which one of the porters had so kindly produced, and pushed him into A&E.

After some 20 minutes, a young doctor examined Hazer's damaged knee. He shook his head. "When did this happen, young man?"

"Yesterday afternoon," Hazer answered.

The doctor shook his head. "Should have come here as soon as it happened."

"I was playing football," Hazer gave his excuse.

"Let's get you to the X-ray department," he said as he waved over a nurse.

The doctor, after examining the X-rays, told Hazer the bad news. His patella was broken and ligaments damaged. He would need an op to repair the damage. "Any questions?" the doctor asked.

Hazer had to ask, "What's the patella?" He thought it was a cigar.

The doctor smiled. "It's your kneecap."

So after putting on a temporary splint plus handed a prescription for painkillers, Hazer was sent home on crutches to await the operation.

A couple of days later, a letter arrived with the date of his hospital admission. It was only a week's time. There was a list attached of what was needed whilst in hospital – slippers and pyjamas were top. Hazer didn't wear jimjams or possess slippers so his mum had to go and buy them or get them on the Provi cheque. (This was a cheque issued by the Provident company for say £20 which you paid back in instalments plus interest.)

The day came. Hazer put his things in a small cardboard suitcase army issue. This included a razor and shaving brush. He only had a few bristles, but it said on the list shaving gear, so he insisted he should have everything on the list.

Jock had to go to work so Hazer and his mum struggled to get the bus to the Royal. Hazer's stomach had caught a thousand butterflies, he couldn't sit still on the bus. On arrival, Hazer's mum had to fill in a form giving her consent to the op.

Then they were shown into an office where a smiling surgeon was sitting reading his notes.

"Ah, Mr Hayes," he said as he stood up. "And this is?" he questioned Hazer.

"Me mum."

"Take a seat, Mrs Hayes." He pulled a chair out from the front of his desk for Hazer's mum to sit down. Hazer thought, "Bloody hell, he's a real gent." Hazer pulled his own chair out and sat next to his mother. Then the surgeon started to explain the op and its consequences. Then the word six to nine months came out. Hazer thought, "Bloody hell, I'll miss the rest of the season."

"It was very nice to meet you, Mrs Hayes," he said as he closed the door. "I'll see you before your operation, John."

So Hazer was admitted to the ward, a bath, then into his new jimjams, helped by a middle-aged nurse who had seen it all before. He had to starve for a day as the deed was done the next morning.

As he lay on top of his bed, the butterflies subsided and he drifted off to the land of nod.

It was 7 in the evening when he was woken by a bell. It was visiting time, one hour every night. It was like being in the nick!

Jock and Aud came in smiling and settled next to Hazer's bed. Jock didn't have much to say, just a grunt in agreement as Aud told Hazer about her day and journey home on the bus and why Jock couldn't have a day off work and take them in the car. Hazer kept looking at the clock, wishing the hand would move faster towards 8.

"Oh, and I bought you a book. It's about spies."

Hazer didn't say much, but looking at the cover it was from *Russia with Love*, by Ian Fleming.

He frowned. Never heard of him.

His mum said, "I know, but it's supposed to be good. The man in the bookshop said so."

The bell rang. Hazer's mum went to give him a kiss, which Hazer dodged.

"Try and be brave," she said.

Hazer thought, "Bloody hell, mum, I'm not going to war."

Jock said, "See yee tomorree."

So it was peaceful once again. Supper was delivered but Hazer was on starvation status. So he opened his book and was introduced to the world of James Bond. He couldn't put this spellbinding book down till lights out at 10:30 pm.

Hazer was awakened by a nurse about 7 am.

"OK, John?" the surgeon stood in front of the bed.

"Yes, sir," Hazer answered.

"You're number 3 on the list, so I'll be operating at about 10 o'clock or so."

Hazer's butterflies returned.

At 9:30 a trolley was brought to the side of Hazer's bed

by a pretty young nurse. On top of the trolley was a bowl of warm, soapy water, a shaving brush and a safety razor.

"Hello John," she said as she gave him a wonderful smile. "I'm going to shave you."

Hazer looked at her with a puzzled face, his whiskers, of which there were few, had been attended by him the previous day.

Hazer scratched his chin as men do when needing a shave. "But I only shaved last night."

The nurse shook her head and gave a little giggle.

"No, not your chin."

Hazer still had not tumbled.

"Your leg."

"Oh my leg!"

"Yes, your leg."

The nurse pulled the curtain around Hazer's bed and pulled back the covers.

"Can you remove your pyjama bottoms please?" she asked politely. Hazer was a bit embarrassed as he was very highly 'you know what' down below.

He struggled to remove his jimjam bottoms.

"Here, let me help," she said as she pulled the legs till they removed, revealing Hazer's Y-fronts plus a bulge to the young nurse.

She never batted an eyelid. She placed a rubber-like blanket under his leg, then foamed up the shaving brush, sploshed Hazer's leg with ample suds and continued to shave his bare limb in the most exotic way.

Hazer had managed to pull a part of the sheet over his underwear, hoping the nurse hadn't noticed his lump. After ten minutes, the curtain opened. Another elderly nurse came in.

"Much longer?" she asked.

"Just about finished, sister," she answered. As she was drying Hazer's leg, he thought she must be her older sibling but didn't ask as he had already dropped one clanger that morning.

"Put your pyjamas back on," the older nurse instructed Hazer in a more superior tone.

Hazer lay back on the bed as the curtains were drawn back. About an hour later (after James Bond had killed the Russian spy in from *Russia with Love*), Hazer was disturbed from his book by a doctor and another nurse. The nurse was carrying a white, what looked like a sheet, with bits of thin cotton string attached. They pulled the curtains round again. "OK John, put this on," the nurse said. "Make sure you take all your clothes off first." She explained how to put it on, so Hazer stripped off (his manhood had returned to normal), placed the sheet over his head and tried to tie the straps at the back, which was impossible.

"Are you decent?" the nurse asked.

"Can't do the bloody thing up."

The nurse poked her head round the curtain. "Most people have the same problem," she said as she entered. "Turnaround and I'll do you up."

Hazer could feel his face brighten as he turned with his bare bottom facing the nurse.

She tied the straps in a bow. "There, all done."

"Thanks," Hazer muttered.

"Now relax. You'll be having a jab in a few minutes."

Hazer lay back on his bed. The butterflies began to invade his stomach once again. The doctor returned about half an hour later with a tray of swabs and the syringe. The injection to help Hazer relax was administered, but rather than relaxing, it made him high. He wanted to get out of bed and spring around the ward like a ballerina, but something deep down stopped him. Ten minutes later the orderly arrived with a trolley. The nurse asked Hazer to lie on the trolley ready to be wheeled to the operating theatre.

Entering the anteroom, Hazer, who was lying on his back, looked up to see the ceiling covered in stars. A doctor came in with a second syringe.

"Hello John, just going to give you a jab to make you sleep." He smiled as he administered the needle in Hazers' arm. "Could you countdown from ten for me?"

Hazer started. "Ten, nine, eight, sev…"

When he woke some four hours later, his mouth felt like an old dishcloth. He was as thirsty as a man stranded on a desert island. He reached for the jug of water which was on the bedside table, then he felt a sharp, agonising pain in his knee. He grimaced. "Shit that hurts," he said under his breath.

But he had to have water, so he stretched again. The pain would have to wait. He guzzled down two large glasses of Adam's ale. Thirst was quenched for a while, so the pain took over his mind. He lay there wondering what his leg looked like, so after half an hour he lifted the bedding and peered down onto his left knee. It was covered in swathes of bandages, held at the side with a safety pin. He tried to move his leg, but the pain was excruciating so he laidback, closed his eyes and tried to sleep. After a while he gave up, opened his eyes and reached for James.

"Good book?" the young nurse inquired.

Hazer nodded.

"What's it called?" she asked as she held out two white tablets.

"*From Russia with Love*," Hazer replied.

"Take these, they will help with the pain," she said as she poured Hazer another glass of water. "Why, you were thirsty, I'll get you another jug."

Hazer swallowed the tablets, returned the glass to the bedside cabinet then returned to his book.

He was gone in the land of dreams.

A bell woke him with a start. He automatically sat up. The pain hit him again. Dinner was being served. It was then Hazer realised how hungry he was. He hadn't eaten for 20 odd hours. A tray was placed in front of him on a small table which sat on the bed. He couldn't sit up and was struggling when the nurse joined him.

"Let me help you, John."

She leaned over Hazer, put her arms under his shirt, shoulders and helped him sit up. The trouble was her breasts were so close to Hazer's nose, the bulge done its thing. His thought was "Well, that's working, thank fuck." This went on for a couple of days then it was decided that Hazer would be moved to Queen Alexandra Hospital for recuperation and physiotherapy. Hazer was put in a wheelchair, pushed to a waiting ambulance and off to the QA.

He was quite sorry he was leaving the Royal as he had grown fond of the young nurse who had administered his care in the last few days.

Hazer was wheeled out of the ambulance and into a long old Nissan Hut lined either side with beds, each with small cabinets alongside. It reminded him of the Dryad cadet holidays.

A male nurse welcomed Hazer, helping him onto his bed. Hazer looked around at his fellow inmates. "Bloody hell," he thought, "they are all as old as the hills." He was on the old age pensioners ward; most of the men were in their declining years.

Hazer settled in and after a couple of days got to know several of the patients. In the next bed was an old boy who had seen it all. Both wars etc. But he never complained; he had one of his legs amputated and was undergoing physio and struggling to walk with crutches. It was Hazer's turn on his third day at the QA. A well-built dark-haired fellow dressed in a tracksuit introduced himself. "My name's Frank and I'm going to be working with you to get you mobile again."

Hazer nodded.

"When are your stitches due out?" he asked.

"Don't know," Hazer answered.

Frank turned away and joined the sister who had a desk to the left of the doorway.

After about ten minutes he came back.

"Tomorrow. I'll see you then."

Hazer was on tenterhooks the next day as two nurses removed his bandages. Looking down, his knee was a blue colour with a multitude of black stitches in a half-moon pattern to the left-hand side. The nurses were having a chat about their boyfriends. They started to cut and pull out the catgut stitching holding Hazer's knee together. The curtain opened and a doctor joined them. He nodded to acknowledge Hazer.

"Let's have a look." he examined Hazer's knee and nodded again. "OK, now it's onto the hard work, young man," he said to Hazer as he drew back the curtains. Hazer lay on the bed. His leg was numb. He struggled to lift it off the sheet, but it hurt like hell that afternoon. Frank joined him. "Let's have a butchers at the damage. Well, that's a nasty one. How did you do it?"

"Football."

He nodded.

"Who did you play for?"

Hazer didn't like 'who did', it suggested his playing days were over.

"Hillside," he replied.

"Well, let's see if we can get you mobile again. Let's try by lifting your leg." Hazer strained. The pain was excruciating, but he managed to lift his leg about two inches.

"Good. Well done, John." Frank was smiling.

He worked with Hazer for about an hour and a half. Hazer had worked up quite a sweat. His jimjam top was soaked.

"How have you been going to the toilet?"

Hazer was embarrassed as he answered. "Bed pan."

"Well I'll get you some crutches tomorrow." With those words, he said his goodbye.

Hazer lay there exhausted, his knee was thumping.

"Here you are, take these." The nurse handed Hazer two white pills." It will help with the pain," she added.

Hazer swallowed the pills, then drifted off in a deep, well-deserved sleep.

"Are yee aweek?" a Glaswegian accent asked as a hand shook his shoulder.

Hazer opened one eye to be confronted by his cousins from the north. Dennis (i.e. Dinky), Jim and Jock all stood dressed in working clothes and smelling of alcohol.

Jim and Dinky sat on the bed eating the fruit Hazer had in the bowl on his dresser.

"How long you been back down?" Hazer asked.

"Come came down on Sunday."

It was now Wednesday. Hazer thought, why didn't Jock mention it? Then he tumbled. They were billeted in his bedroom.

Shit that's it, no more privacy, he smiled as the thought ran through his head.

"How you been doing. How you been, Dinky," Hazer asked.

"Alreet, Uncle John's got me a job with the plumber." (Dinky had been an apprentice plumber in Scotland.) He always called Jock 'Uncle John', as did Jim and all the other visitors from God's country, as Jock called it.

The bell rang. Visiting time was over.

"See yee tomorree," Jim said as he peeled the last orange from Hazer's now empty bowl.

Hazer nodded. "Yea, see yah."

Hazer had his supper which was always accompanied by a half bottle of beer, either a milk stout or Guinness. Hazer got to like the taste of Guinness and in later years it was his tipple of choice.

He had been holding on for about an hour but he had to go.

He caught the attention of one of the nurses.

"Can I have a bedpan?" he whispered.

"No problem."

She returned with a silver metal bedpan. Hazer had been having difficulty lifting his bum onto the pan in the past, but this night was the accident waiting to happen.

The nurse pulled the curtain around and left Hazer to his own devices. He pulled his jimjams down to his knees, rolled over and pushed the pan under his backside. As he did this, he farted and shite himself at the same time. The smell was enough to kill an elephant. The mess was everywhere. Hazer was so so embarrassed.

"Nurse!" he shouted out. "Nurse!"

The nurse put her head round the curtain.

"Ha! Had an accident, have we? Don't worry."

Two minutes later ,the nurse and one of her junior colleagues came through the curtains with bowls of water and cleaning agents.

They cleaned Hazer up, removing all the soiled bedding, remade the bed and settled Hazer back down, all within half an hour. After that, Hazer was determined never to use a bedpan again. Never ever.

The days went on. Hazer was working hard with Frank and he was devouring every James Bond book. He got to know George, his one-legged mate in the next bed, exchanging stories, Hazer about his school days and football, George about his time in the Navy.

Hazer was on his feet and able to bend his knee a little after eight days, so he was discharged from the QA with a pair of crutches, but had to come back for physio two hours every weekday. He said his goodbyes to the nurses; he had already thanked Frank for all his hard work. Then when it came to his mate in the next bed a lump came to his throat. He had grown really fond of his old matelot friend and would miss his stories and banter. George was a real man.

Losing the crutches and my job

Aud had walked round to escort Hazer home from the QA hospital. Hazer was embarrassed as she went to give him a hug and kiss.

"Don't mum," he whispered. "Everyone's looking."

His mum took a step back and smiled, then reached down to pick up a small case that held Hazer's hospital attire.

"Dad's at work," she wanted to explain.

"Don't worry, I'm OK," Hazer answered.

As he turned to wave goodbye to the nurses and fellow patients of the Nissan Hut that had been his home for the last week or so, he pushed the swing doors open with his back and re-entered the world with part of his kneecap, which was in a jar in his pocket.

He got home to his new shared bedroom with Dinky and Jim.

"I'll make you a nice cuppa," his mum said, almost apologetically for him having to share a bedroom again.

"It's OK, Mum. Don't worry, I'll sleep on the sofa till I get rid of these." Hazer raised one of the crutches. He couldn't wait till 6 o'clock and meeting his mates for the visit to Hillside.

Hazer struggled to have a strip wash as a bath was out of the question, but he had to look his best for the Hillside girls. The Brylcreem was plastered on his jet-black hair. It was hard to get his Elvis quiff right with him trying to balance on one crutch. He looked in the mirror and thought to himself that will have to do.

He joined the gang at the bars, catching up on all the gossip, mostly about girls and what they had got up to (mostly white lies) and the conquests they had with each girl mentioned.

It was 'I had her at the back of the flats' or 'I had her down the path'. All to be taken with a pinch of salt as the gang had a vivid imagination when it came to girls.

Hillside was always quiet on a Monday night after the hectic weekend. Ernie was his usual self, a cigarette in his four-fingered hand as he greeted the gang at the door.

"Alright, boys?"

"Yeah, Ern," the boys answered.

Hazer hobbled past Ernie to pay his subs. Ernie waved him away. Hazer put his two bob back in his pocket.

"Cheers. Ern."

Ernie just nodded.

It was three weeks since Hazer had entered the hallowed hall of Hillside. His eyes were all about for new talent (i.e. girls). One girl caught his eye, but she was a bit younger so he pushed her to the back of his mind.

"Want a game of snooker?" It was Lenny, the older boy who had been friendly whilst playing football out the back.

"Don't think I'll be able to hold the cue."

"That's why I asked. I'm shit and you could be the only one I can beat."

They both laughed. The smile on Lenny's face seemed to light up the room. Hazer duly lost at snooker but found a friend – more on that in the next books.

"Want a coffee?" Lenny asked.

"Yeah, alright."

So the two new companions went down the stairs to the newly opened coffee bar built by the boys.

"This is Frankie." Lenny introduced Hazer to this tall, gangly lad, maybe three years older than Hazer.

"Alright, mush?" Hazer asked.

"Yeah," Frankie replied.

"You done a bit of boxing, I hear."

"Yeah, not much."

"I never learned to duck."

"Nor did I." They both laughed. The small coffee bar was filling up. Then someone said, "Lights are on." The signal for the boys to exit on the five-a-side football battle that occurred four nights a week at Hillside.

Hazer was left alone at the bar with just his crutches for company. He was feeling sorry for himself when Peggy pushed another cup of coffee his way.

"Thanks, Peg."

"Drink it up. You'll be alright."

Hazer sipped his coffee, watching the lads kick the shit out of each other on that small tarmacked piece of heaven that was Hillsides five-a side– or 12-a-side – tarmac.

The night ended. Hazer and his mates made their way home, singing all the popular songs of the time, Teddy, as usual, completely out of tune.

"Had a good night?" Hayes's mum asked.

"Yeah, alright. I'm going to sleep on the sofa."

Hazer couldn't handle going to bed and sharing with Dinky and Jim. They fidgeted like hell. Hazer lay on the sofa. His head was twirling. He couldn't get this young girl out of his mind.

"You alreet son?" a broad Glasgow accent filled the room. Jim stood shaking Hazer awake. It was 6 o'clock. The cousins were off to work with Jock.

"Fuck me, Jim."

"Sorry, dinee meen tah week yea."

Hazer thought, "Then why the fuck did you?" Jim had a broad smile on his mush.

"Yea'll be back ta work in na tame," he added.

Hazer just nodded as teenagers do, then rolled back over

and returned to the dream that was good, but he couldn't remember how good.

Living with crutches was so so boring. Hazer every morning would get up and walk or hobble down to Cosham, or to be succinct Milly's cafe. Every day he would meet a host of young men waiting to get a day's work, each one in Milly's waiting for a subbie (a self-employed contractor) to pick them out for a day's work.

But Kenny, who had his sarnies everyday care of his mum and a packet of fags, care of same mum, was always sat on the sill of the window. Hazer got to know Kenny over at Hillside so to find him at Milly's at 7:30 am was unique. It was like the Red Indian cigar man you see outside American stores. Always there, he would tell his mum and dad he was going to work, take his sarnies, fags and sit outside Milly's until it was time to go home, but he was a brill footballer – missed his vocation.

Milly's was like Hillside but for grown-ups. The characters were out of comic books for the oppressed, but they weren't oppressed. They were funny, loyal and genuine.

"How's your leg?" Freddy asked. He was one of Jock's mates.

"Alright, Fred," Hazer answered. Freddy was a true gentleman. A laugh a minute.

Freddy was sitting with his cold empty cup trying to keep warm by the paraffin heater.

"Fucking freezing innit?" he gestured Hazer to the heater.

"Want a cuppa, Fred?" Hazer asked.

"Nah. keep your money, son."

"Come on, looks like you could."

"Nah, keep your money, son."

Freddy knew his horses. That was his thing. When horses and carts went out and cars took over, he was lost. Hazer sat with Freddy and Kenny the Indian for the next three weeks, listening to Freddy's stories and watching Kenny dodge into the alley if anybody who was acquainted to his mum was on the horizon.

Freddy was at the time sleeping in Johnny Gregory's lorry at the back of Cosham library. He lived there for three years, but he never ever was grumpy.

Milly's was a meeting place after the pubs had shut, which was 2:30 on a Saturday afternoon. Hazer had been having a pint in the George. His crutches made him look older than he was.

"Going up Milly's?" Austin asked.

Hazer had had six brown splits, so he was a little unsteady on his crutches.

"Yeah," Hazer answered.

The boys went up to Milly's, all of them half pissed.

"I'll have one of your delicious steak pies, Mother," Hazer said in a semi-drunken voice. Everyone called Mrs Graham 'Mother'.

Everyone from the pubs of Cosham went to Milly's till the pubs reopened at 6 o'clock. There used to be a blind man who was a regular visitor to Cosham, and every one of Hazer's mates would help him across the road outside of Milly's where a zebra crossing was. This day the blind man was coming along, his white stick waving ahead of him. Everyone who had been in the pub was now outside of Milly's. The blind man appeared. Everyone was expecting Ralphie, who took his hand, to see him across the zebra crossing. Instead, he took him to the middle of the roundabout and left him there. He was twisting around with his white stick. Hazer looked on. It was s stupid, but at the time there was no traffic, and it made some of them laugh. The gentleman was rescued and they would never have let anything happen to him, but that was

Ralphie fucking idiot.

"This hurts."

"It's supposed to."

"Bend your knee."

Hazer's eyes were full of pain.

"Frank, it hurts like fuck."

Hazer's knee was swollen, scarred, and as sore as he could stand.

"You want to play again?"

"Yeah."

"Well bend your knee."

So it was hard work, but if he wanted to play football again, this was the only way.

"Hazer, you alright?" Ernie asked.

"Yeah."

"Right, let's go."

The boys entered Fratton Park. The final of the Lads League Cup. Hazer had done it. He had managed to get there. Every football player's dreams of playing on the sacred ground of their hometown club.

"Fuck me, Jock. We're gonna be late."

"Don't worry, we'll have you there on time."

Fratton Park. The home of football.

"Yes, he is playing," Ronny August said.

As the man on the players' entrance shook his head. "Go and get Ernie."

"Who's fucking Ernie?" he questioned.

"Our manager, you fucking wanker."

Hazer had lost his lot.

Trying to get back fighting, struggling to be fit again, there to miss the chance to play on the hallowed turf of Fratton Park. The game was good at first. 3–0 up but Highland Rovers fought back. No excuses, but they poisoned the keeper,

Barry Houghton, so he was fucked so Ernie in his wisdom recruited a boy called Budgie (he had a large nose). The game progressed. They were 4–0 at half time (Gadders, Upsall, Raff and Hazer). Then it was the sunset turned to dust every time they entered the box. The boy who should have been in a cage let the ball in the first through his legs. We won the league and nobody went to Duisburg.

Me, college and the dockyard depart

Hazer was still at college, recovered from his knee injury, but his mates were all on the buildings earning three or four times his wages, even though Jock subsidised him. He wasn't happy. He wanted to earn big bucks like his mates.

It was exam time. City and Guilds at Flathouse Quay. Hazer had missed three months out with his knee, so in reality he shouldn't have been expected to take this exam as he was three months behind his classmates.

The hall was the same as when he was taking the entrance exam. Long lines of simple desks. The tutors stood at the rear of each line. The exam began. Hazer, although missing many weeks of study, was finding it quite easy. He had done the first two pages and was in the third or fourth after about an hour and a half. Sat in front was Billy Best. They were talking about the up-and-coming football season when they would be entering men's football. All of a sudden a clipboard thwacked against the back of Hazer's nut.

Hazer jumped up. "What the fuck was that for?"

"Cheating," came the answer from the middle-aged six-foot-tall, square-shouldered assassin.

"I wasn't fucking cheating, you wanker." Hazer was going into full attack mode.

With that, the assassin grabbed Hazer by the lapel. This was the worst thing he could have done. Hazer's instinct for survival took over. His forehead acted like a battering ram against his assailant's nose, which exploded with blood. Snot gushing from it, he staggered back, but there was nowhere to go but the floor. Hazer stood still, his fists clenched, ready for any more attackers.

"Fuck me, Hazer, you've done it now," Bestie whispered in Hazer's ear. Hazer nodded, picked up his papers, which were splattered with blood and snot, took them to the front desk, and handed them in. The hall was in complete silence.

Hazer faced the man behind the desk." I wasn't cheating." He spoke in a calm, low voice, knowing his dockyard and his dreams of travelling the world with the Merchant Navy were over.

The police got involved, but as the instructor had struck the first blow, it was decided not to prosecute Hazer for assault. Hazer breathed a sigh of relief when the sergeant behind the desk informed Hazer, who had been summoned to Portsmouth police station, that he was in the clear.

Hazer had told his mum but never had the bottle to tell Jock. All week he was trying to get Jock in a good mood before he informed him.

It was 6 am on the Monday morning. Jim and Dinky had left Hazer in the land of dreams as they went downstairs to get washed before going to work.

"I'm drowning!" Hazer screamed.

"Get out of that bed now," Jock shouted. "Get that working gear on."

Hazer had jumped out of bed, which was soaked, care of the saucepan of cold water delivered by Jock.

"So you want to be on the buildings, bloody idiot?" Jock wasn't a happy bunny.

"Wasting all that?" he stopped in mid-sentence. "Get doo the stairs, grab a cuppa, you got five minutes to get into Ronny's van."

Ronny August had a Ford Dormobile work-a-bus. It had two seats in the front with bench seats either side, it was capable of carrying another ten men.

Hazer rushed down the stairs, grabbed a mug of tea, pulled his boots on and was out the door joining Jim, Dinky and the rest of the gang who Hazer knew from his Saturday exploits.

"You've upset the old man," Ronny August shook his head as he closed the sliding doors.

The blokes never said a word, just sitting there looking straight ahead like zombies knowing they had another week of backbreaking toil ahead of them, with no hope of respite unless they won the pools.

This was the world Hazer had chosen, but he had to stick it out. He wouldn't give in.

The gangs split up. "You go with Boomer, Ronny, Bernie digging footings."

This was the hardest work and Jock had put Hazer to the test. The foundations were two feet wide and three feet deep. All hand dug or if you came across flint, or any other hard ground, pick and shovel.

Hazer was placed with Ronny bottoming up. This was shovelling any dirt left in the trench after a fork was used to excavate a spit deep (a spit being the depth of the prongs on the fork), everything done was loaded into a wheelbarrow and pushed 30 yards away from the foundation. The wheelbarrows were on scaffold planks of wood, as it was impossible to push through the mud. This was backbreaking work. Hazer's hands were like pieces of rag with the popped blisters dangling.

"Piss on them." The advice came from Teddy Pinmore who Hazer had watched playing football alongside Jock when he was a lad.

"What?" Hazer was dumbfounded.

"Piss on them." Teddy was insistent.

So Hazer, the next time he went to the thunder box with the hole dug underneath to catch the excrement, peed all over his hands and rubbed it in. It stung like fuck, but after a few days the pain was reduced to what was bearable.

Hazer's mum was always trying to help Hazer with his hands, but he wouldn't give in. Hazer, after a couple of months, was given a new task – jointing pipes. This involved pushing yarn (tarred) into the corners of the pipes, then knocking up sand and cement at the right ratio (if you got this wrong they would leak). Then tucking and jointing, finishing with a trowelled edge. Then after the joints had hardened, a water test was put on the run. If any leaks appeared, the line failed and the gang wouldn't get paid. So it was on Hazer's head to make sure they never leaked.

Sometimes in the summer the joints would dry out too quick and a small crack would appear. To remedy this, hundreds of used cement bags were placed in a water butt and when soaked placed over each joint to stop it drying out too quick. So in the summer months, while the rest of the gang were having a break, Hazer was like a bee buzzing around making sure the bags were wet or he was to blame if the men had a deduction in their money for leaking pipes.

Driving test

Hazer had been driving on the sites and new estate roads for a couple of years. He was now 17 and a proper learner's licence was acquired, so he was legal at last. A set of L plates were attached to Jock's new Ford Zodiac.

So Hazer had the run of the road as Jock didn't care if he was still a learner driver. He would handover the keys, only going to run so and so home Hazer would plead.

After a few weeks with Kenny Wearn beside him, Hazer had gotten used to the Zodiac, though he had to sit on a cushion to see over the steering wheel. So he applied for his test full of confidence.

The day came. They were working in Guildford, so Hazer drove to Pompey with Kenny by his side, ready to blitz the test. He failed, speeding 32 mph in a 30 mile per hour limit. Hazer drove back to Guildford sick as a sick person. Kenny explained they were never going to let him pass in the Zodiac. He would need to go to a driving school, borrow their car for the test. Hazer took Kenny's advice, went to the British School of Motoring, took the lessons, used their car for the test and passed all within six weeks for failing his first one.

So he was now a fully-fledged driver with Jock's Zodiac to boot. This was a bird magnet, or so Hazer thought.

Weekdays seemed to drag. Digging, laying pipes, concreting – it was never ending, but at the end of the week, the crisp pound notes which Jock dealt out to the men seemed worth the struggle. Jock would spend Friday from lunchtime in the pub with the rest of his workforce, often getting the lock-in. It was Hazer's job to drive Jock and a couple of men back to Pompey. So Friday was more often than not spent hanging around on site waiting till 4 o'clock, then picking up the half-sloshed retinue, transferring them to the Ship in Cosham to continue drinking till the pubs closed. Then it was the carry-out cases of booze to be drunk till the early hours in Jock's front room. The routine was carried out every Friday.

It was on one Friday that Hazer got to know this bloke. He was ugly. He had a nose like a nose that had never been seen out of the animal kingdom. His chin was like the back of a double decker bus after an accident, shoulders and build of her gorilla but his wit and charisma was magnetic to Hazer and his mates. His name was Brian Madden. He was an ex-Coldstream Guardsman, and a laugh a minute, but when he was pissed, the biggest pest in Cosham by a mile.

He had just moved up to Wymering and was working alongside Raff and Plummy as a plasterers' labourer, whilst the two of them were learning their trade. An example of his humour was retold by Plummy. They were working away putting the first coat of plaster on the wall (sand and cement). As they were trainees, they weren't very good. Madden came up the stairs with a large hod which was used to transfer the muck (sand and cement) from the mixer to the spot board where the plasterers took a hawkful to proceed to spread it up the wall. Madden entered the room and tipped the muck from the hod all over the floor. Plummy and Raff looked at each other, a puzzled look on their faces. Madden turned round and left the two bewildered would-be plasterers flummoxed. They looked at each other. Madden returned and did the same thing, tipping the muck on the floor.

Plummy had to ask, "What you doing that for?" Brian Madden looked at them, then said, "Well, that's where it ends up."

The two looked at each other. Brian Madden was right, a third of the muck, which should have been attached to the wall, was attached to the floor. This was Madden's wit or sarcasm they learned. They had to be cleaner at the job, lesson learned.

Football season/the end of Hazer's football youth

The lads had gotten into a routine – piss-up on a Friday night, up at 8 am, go for a swim in the new Victoria baths swimming pool situated next to the Guildhall to sober up, then breakfast, a large fry-up in the Richmond Grill. Then pubs were open and it was back on the lash. Then at lunchtime, closing 2:30 pm. It was sit around in Woolie's cafe till opening time.

"Can I borrow the car? Got footy today."

"Aye, but you'll have't put some petrol in." Jock was fed up with Hazer using all his petrol. Though the money to Jock was irrelevant, he wanted to instil in Hazer the dictum 'nought for nought in this world'.

Hazer pulled up at the small petrol station behind Paulsgrove shops. "Two gallons please."

The petrol pump attendant delivered the two gallons to perfection. Hazer always wondered why he never ever went over the mark. Hazer still can't get the measure right. Hazer handed the attendant a crisp pound note and received a ten bob note back, five shillings a gallon. Or as Hazer thought four brown splits (bottle of Brickwoods brown ale) and half a pint of mild in a pint glass. If you had a good barman or maid they would give you three-quarters of a pint of mild instead of half, so you gained a quarter of a pint. The old boys of the Clacton had informed Hazer of this when he first started drinking there.

He pushed the petrol cap back on, got the receipt to prove to Jock that he had indeed filled up. He asked the attendant for a ticket for four gallons, not two.

He plumped up the cushion so he could get over the steering wheel, then preceded to pick the lads up. Gadders was first then Upsall and lastly Raff.

"We going swimming first?" Gadders asked, holding a towel alongside his football boots.

Hazer nodded, pointing to the towel on the seat next to him. Gadders put both his and Hazer's towels on the rear window space and joined Hazer on the front bench seat.

"What happened last night? I was blotto, can't remember a thing."

"You can't remember Madden eating the goldfish?"

Gadders looked on, a puzzled look on his curly-headed face.

"He what?"

"Swallowed the goldfish."

"Was that in the Indian?"

"Yeah, you remember."

"Nah, not really."

What happened the previous night…

"I fancy a curry." Madders was always up for a curry, never paid. Always done a runner.

The boys who had been with Brian on a pub crawl down Lance Road were three sheets to the wind.

"Alright, I'm starving," Raff piped up.

Hazer nodded in agreement. Teddy said, "Don't mind." Plummy shrugged, Austin and Gadders were out of it.

They had ended up in the Richmond, a pub where Brian Madden was the star at singing, telling jokes, mimicking, taking off famous people and a bit of dancing. He was a born entertainer until he had one over the eight. Then he was like Doctor Jekyll and Mr Hyde. A pest, as stated before.

That night he was on his best behaviour after he had entertained the audience.

"A new one's opened on the corner of Sussex Road, we ain't done a runner from there."

So it was agreed. Don't go in altogether, two at a time and sit separately and by the door if possible, ready to run. Hazer and Austin found a seat by the door. The others were situated around this new establishment. The waiters were busy taking orders, ignoring Brian, who was getting frustrated by the wait. He stood up after some 20 minutes, went to the counter on which was a large fish tank with a multitude of coloured fish, swimming about enjoying the evening ambiance.

"Please sit down, sir, we won't be long," one of the waiters pleaded.

Madden shook his head, then rolled his sleeves up. Hazer thought he was going to whack the waiter, but he sunk his arm into the fish tank, caught a coloured fish, held it up and swallowed it. Hazer and his mates couldn't believe what they had witnessed as Madden went fishing again. The waitress started screaming something in her own language; she was joined by four more gentlemen from the kitchen, armed to the teeth with knives, long knives and longer knives.

Madden thought the better part of valour and skedaddled out the front door.

Hazer looked at Austin. "Don't think we'll do a runner out of here," so they forgot about food and discreetly left the restaurant followed by their mates. They put that restaurant in the memory box. Don't do a runner from there.

They picked Upsall and Raff up. Raff was telling Upsall the story of a goldfish as they journeyed to the baths.

After a refreshing swim, it was the Richmond for breakfast. Just as they were leaving, Madden came through the door, a big smile on his ugly mug.

"Alright, Brian?" Hazer inquired.

"Nah, got gut ache."

Raff laughed, then sang, "It wriggled and wriggled inside ya." Madden grinned as he rubbed his belly.

"Want a cuppa to wash goldie down?" Upsall was laughing.

"Nah pubs be open soon. Think I'll have a pint. What you lot up to?"

"First game of the season," Gadders sparked up.

"Where you playing?"

"I'm at Bransbury, Hazer, Raff, Upsall is at Farlington," Gadders replied.

"What time's kick-off?"

"3 o'clock," Hazer kicked in.

"You've loads of time. Fancy a pint?" Madden was tempting them.

"Nah, we're playing."

"Just a shandy won't hurt."

"Alright, suppose it won't hurt, just one."

So to the Richmond they went. Hazer parked up outside. No, yellow lines those days. No cars either.

The pub was just filling up, everyone trying to down the first pint after Friday's beanfeast. That first pint always took 20 minutes to sink.

"What you want?" Madden asked.

"Only a shandy." Gadders' head was still banging.

"Here, try one of these." Madden held up a small greenish coloured bottle.

"What is it?" Raff asked.

"Carlsberg Special it's non-alcoholic." Madden smiled, knowing it was far from non-alcoholic but potent to the extreme.

"Yeah, alright, we'll try one." Hazer had just dug his footballing grave.

"I'll have another one of those," Gadders said. "It's helping my headache."

"I'll join you."

"So will I."

"Want another?"

"Why not."

"Want one more?"

"Yeah, alright."

"One for the road.?"

"Alright."

"Fuck me. Look at the time?" Gadders slurred

Hazer looked at the clock above the bar – nearly 2 o'clock. He saw more than two hands and several numbers too many.

"We gotta go, Brian."

So Hazer, who was half pissed, and his three drunken mates, left Brian and drove to Bransbury Park. Gadders tripped as he got out of the car.

"See-ee you later," he mumbled.

It was up the Eastern Road, Hazer driving as carefully as he could manage without hitting the curb. Luckily there were hardly any cars on the roads in those days. They pulled into Farlington car park, made their way to the pavilion to be greeted by Ernie, who was looking at his watch. "You're late, hurry up and get changed."

The three half-pissed players struggled to get into the boots and kit, giggles leaving their lips now and again.

"We'd better sober up," Hazer thought. "That wanker, Madden, must have spiked our non-alcoholic drinks. So him, Raff and Upsall went to the showers and doused themselves in cold water.

The team talk was brief.

"Right boys, this is men's football. You won't be able to bully the other sides. In fact, you will be bullied by other sides. So go out and do your best." Ernie delivered this speech like Churchill, only no cigar, just a fag in his four-fingered hand.

The first 20 minutes were a blur. Hazer started to come round, as did Raff and Upsall, then Raff scored, on 25 minutes, followed by Mossy Merran, 2–0 up.

The ball went over the top. Hazer ran into it. 3–0. This is easy, Hazer thought.

Now in those days you could barge the goalkeeper shoulder to shoulder to try and make him drop the ball. It was within the laws of the game. The ball went over Hazer's head. The keeper never quite had a grip on it, when Hazer in his wisdom decided to go shoulder to shoulder with him – well, more like shoulder to waist as he was over 6 foot and Hazer was 5 foot 3. The keeper took umbrage to his little assailant and grabbed him by the shirt, swinging him around like a ragdoll. Hazer managed to regain his foothold and swung a left hook under the keeper's chin. He reeled back, then was about to send Hazer to the QA hospital when Raff got in front and sent him to the turf with a perfect short jab. This was the signal for all-out war. The young boys of Hillside versus these men. There was blood and snot everywhere. Even Ernie waded in, pretending to break it up, but delivering the odd blow to the boys' adversaries. The problem was the referee, who was also trying to disentangle the fighting teams, was knocked out by who no one to this day knows, but Hazer and Raff got the blame. So ended Hazer's first game in men's soccer. He was banned and never graced a football pitch in Hampshire for five years. Raff was allowed back after two years.

Camouflage

It was a normal Saturday morning, swimming, breakfast, a few pints, then Millys Cafe. Sometimes young ladies would pop upstairs for a coffee break during their shopping excursions. The lads would always try to chat them up, but alas weren't very successful, but this day Hazer pulled, giving this young girl some bullshit about his dad owning a nightclub called the Starlight, meaning Portsdown Hill. She was hooked as Hazer promised he could get her a job.

"Boys, I'll see you later," Hazer said as he held the young lady's hand.

"Where you going?" Madden asked.

"Taking this young lady up the Starlight Club," Hazer winked at his mates.

"We'll come. You can drop us off at the George," Teddy laughed as he knew he was putting the block in.

Hazer couldn't say no. So Madden, Teddy and Plummy joined Hazer and his new-found friend.

"You lot get in the back and I'll drop you off." Hazer wasn't too happy.

The young lady sat in the front seat and put her hand on Hazer's knee. He thought, "I'm in here" then looking in the rear-view mirror glimpsed his mates with wicked grins on their faces.

"OK, you lot, out you get."

"See you later," Teddy said.

Hazer waited for them to enter the pub, then put the car in gear and drove to the car park by the fort on top of Portsdown Hill, about half a mile from the pub.

They sat for a while then started to snog.

"You fancy a walk?" Hazer smiled after coming up for air.

"Yeah, don't mind."

So they left the car hand in hand. Hazer's other hand held an old blanket retrieved from the back seat.

They found a quiet spot surrounded by long grass. Hazer lay the blanket down on the slope of Portsdown Hill. He sat down. She joined him. They continued snogging. Hazer was holding back; he had a strange feeling they were not alone.

He looked up and an ugly mug leaning on his elbows, disguised in tufts of grass, was looking at him no more than three feet away. Madden was grinning. Hazer's head turned. There were Plummy and Teddy, both covered in straw camouflage, lying on the other side.

"You bastards!" Hazer was wild, repeating, "You fucking wankers."

The poor girl nearly had a heart attack. Madden, Plummy and Teddy started to laugh thinking it was a joke. But Hazer rightly copted the needle.

"I'm so sorry." He was trying to calm the young lady down. "I'll take you home." He felt so guilty.

The journey back to Pompey was in complete silence. Hazer had always wondered what happened to this young lady and if she could ever forgive him. Apparently Madden, who had been in the army, covered the other two and himself in straw, then they had crawled more than 200 yards through the long grass to spy on Hazer, the bastards.

The explosion

It was a normal Saturday. The boys had foregone the swimming and were in Milly's cafe waiting for the George and Dragon to open, drinking tea and playing on the pin tables. The trick to get numerous replays had been carried out, whilst Mother (Mrs Graham) wasn't looking, i.e. the two cups were placed upside down, under the two front legs, levelling the machine. This made the ball get stuck in a point scoring hole, thus stopping the scoring to get the replays, so saving the lads a tanner a go.

Teddy had got a job on the council alongside Ralphie. They had to work on a Saturday morning and after their shift would join the lads in the pub. The council had a depot behind Milly's cafe.

The gang were cheering each other on about the scoring on the pinball tables when *bang*, "What the fuck was that?" Ronny Rolf exclaimed, whilst trying to stop the ball going down the hole.

"Fuck knows," old Freddy Ware was shaking his head. Tea had spilled down his front as the noise gave him a shock.

The place went silent for a minute or two, then the door flew open and Teddy rushed in, a scarf wrapped around his head covering his lower face.

"What's up, Ted?" Austin asked.

"I blew him up! He's gonna kill me." Teddy was panicking. It looked like he was going to shit himself in the middle of the café.

"You'll have to hide me away."

The boys were all looking rather bemused.

Then Mother joined them. "What's happened?" she asked. Like a mother hen, she looked out for her boys.

"I blew him up."

"Who did you blow up?" she asked shaking Teddy's shoulders.

"Ralphie." Teddy gave a little squeak.

"He's gonna murder me, honest Mother, please."

"Come on, get down the stairs." She ushered Teddy down the stairs and out of harm's way.

Milly's was a proper restaurant years before, with kitchens downstairs, a seating area upstairs, and a dumb waiter to boot.

The lads carried on playing on the pinball machines when the door opened. Ralphie stood there. His hair was still sizzling, what was left of it. His coat was still smouldering, little puffs of smoke coughed up from his burnt, charred boots. His nose was peeling its skin, his eyebrows and eyelashes were no more.

"I'm gonna kill him."

Georgie Thorpe, one of the funniest men to come from Cosham, inquired, "Something wrong, John?" (Ralphie's first name.)

"I've just been blown up for fuck's sake."

Thorpie stood back, looked Ralphie up and down, and said, "You can't come to the pub like that."

Ralphie shook his head.

"Where the fuck is he?"

"Who?"

"Fucking Teddy."

"Ain't seen him." George kept a straight face but deep down he was laughing his head off. The rest were trying not to burst out laughing. It was Ralphie's justice for the blind man. JR (that's another of Ralphie's nicknames) realised he was getting nowhere so turned and left.

As soon as he closed the door, laughter erupted.

"Has he gone?" Teddy crept back into the cafe proper.

"Yeah, he's gone. What the fuck happened?" Freddy Ware was dying to know, as were the rest of Milly's customers. So Teddy went on to explain.

They had a bet – ten bob – that they could stay in the elephant (this was an aluminium structure, about ten-foot long by four-foot wide, shaped like a round-top tent, it had bench seats on each side and was used as a tea hut. It never had a door) the longest with the gas bottle on, no flame. So they geared themselves up, wet their clothes, placed soaking wet scarves around their heads, then turned the gas on. After a few minutes, the gas was building up, Teddy's eyes were starting to water. Ralphie was Ralphie, staring Teddy out.

So Teddy started to crack. He couldn't stand it any longer, so conceded defeat, but on his way out lit a match and threw it at JR. Just as he was exiting the elephant, the explosion and fireball threw Ralphie in the air. Teddy shit himself and ran like hell to be rescued by Mrs Graham.

JR got his ten bob.

Bachelor night at The Albany

Terry Upsall was courting a young girl called Katie and not taking any precautions. The inevitable happened – she fell pregnant so a wedding was arranged. Hazer was asked to be Terry's best man. He agreed, but weddings weren't like nowadays. It was registry office, then home for a cup of tea.

The bachelor night was always the best bit, so meeting in the Clacton it was decided to go down the town. The boys had a few pints, then piled into Hazer's (Jock's) car.

The first stop was the Richmond where Brian Madden was onstage, taking off James Cagney. 'You dirty rat' was his punchline.

Madden joined the boys at the bar after his set.

"What's the occasion?" he asked.

"Upsall's bachelor night," Hazer answered.

"Where you going?"

"Don't know," Hazer answered, not lifting his head. "Might do the town." This consisted of the Albany, Lennox, Criterion, Railway public houses. All packed to the rafters with sailors – and where there were sailors, there were prostitutes.

Always a laugh a minute as every weekend in the Albany a punch-up would evolve amongst the matelots and the barman and Bruno Errington (who he nicknamed Batman and Robin), a professional wrestler who would happen to wade in to break up the warring factions.

The boys decided to visit the Albany and within half an hour it erupted. There were sailors fighting sailors, customers joining in. It was like a John Wayne movie with Batman and Robin joined by the Jolly Green Giant. Bruno was six foot nine inches at least, trying to calm the situation.

Hazer and his mates just stood back and enjoyed this weekly spectacle.

"Come on, let's piss off."

"Yes, seen enough," Upsall said as a beer glass whizzed past his head, smashing against the wall behind him.

The boys left the boozer, got into Jock's car and hunted for an Indian restaurant they hadn't done runner from.

"We ain't been in here" Raff said as he had a squint around the door.

"They ain't got any goldfish," Austin laughed.

Madden just grinned.

So the gang entered two by two, separated by ten minute intervals.

They behaved like proper gentleman, always saying 'thank you' or 'please may I…' emphasising the 'please', when they had had their fill. The signal was given. It was always after you had asked the waiter for the bill. He thought you were going to pay, but as soon as he returned to the register to get your bill, quite often with his back to you, you just stood up and walked out as nonchalantly as was possible. Then as soon as they left the establishment, they ran like hell.

"What we going to do now?" someone asked.

"Jock will have a carry-out, if you fancy it."

"Yeah, alright."

So the gang decided to visit Hazer's and drink Jock's beer.

"Alright Jock." The boys introduced themselves.

"Beers oo'er there," Jock said, as he pointed to a crate full of Brickwood brown ales.

The boys helped themselves and sat around the room listening to Jock and his mates trying to sing. It was awful. Hazer looked at Terry. He was turning a canary yellow colour.

"You alright, mate?"

"Nah, feel sick as a dog," he answered as his throat started to fill with the curry he had just devoured. With that, he stood up, run outside, and deposited his ill-gotten gains all over the backyard.

"That's better," he said as Hazer joined him.

"Want another beer?"

"Yeah, why not."

So the night went on, everyone drifting home in dribs and drabs, Upsall and BG said "Goodnight", each trying to hold each other up.

"Hang on, I'll get you home," Hazer said.

But it was too late. The pair of them were fast asleep on the sofa.

"You better leave him to sleep it off," Plummy said as he staggered out the door.

The next morning, Hazer came downstairs to find Upsall and BG had gone home through the night. After all, Upsall was getting married at 11:30 am at Pompey registry office.

"What's the time, Hazer?" asked his mum.

"9:30," she answered.

"Shit, I'm going to be late."

Hazer rushed to get ready, jumped in Jock's car and was at Terry's front door by 10:30 am, looking as dapper as was possible. The door opened. Terry stood there looking like a zombie.

"I'm really ill," he whispered.

"Come on or we'll be late," Hazer said.

Upsall shook his head trying to sober up. Then he tried to smile. Hazer looked at him. Something wasn't right.

"Here, I'll help you with that tie."

Then, as Hazer was tightening Terry's tie in a Windsor knot, he then tumbled what was wrong.

"Your tooth," he exclaimed.

Terry stood still, his tongue exploring the gap in his front teeth.

"Fuck. I've lost my tooth!" he shouted out. "Can't get married without me tooth!"

Hazer's mind went back to the previous time Terry had lost his treasured molar. It was at a party up at KB's house in the winter of '63. They found his treasured incisor frozen in his last meal in KB's back garden. Terry had then boiled a kettle, poured it over his regurgitated dinner, extracted his tooth, and replaced it in his then gapped front.

"I know where they are," Hazer laughed.

Upsall looked puzzled.

"You were sick in our backyard. Remember?"

Upsall raised his eyebrows and blew out through his gap.

"Can't remember."

"Come on or we'll be late."

So it was back to number 9.

"What you two doing back? You'll be late." Aud sounded quite concerned.

"He's lost his tooth."

"He's what?"

"His tooth," Hazer repeated, "but I think I know where it is."

So into the backyard the two young men ventured. Jock's backyard was like the Amazon jungle. The grass or weeds with three feet high.

"Here it is," Hazer pointed down to a vindaloo. Peas and potato bhaji, naan bread and copious amounts of stale brown ale, on top of which sat a false tooth, a bit like a tiara on the head of an Indian princess.

Terry was nearly sick again.

Hazer's mum was at the back door. "You boys alright?"

"We found his tooth but it's covered in gunk."

Aud went back indoors and brought a bowl of soapy water. “Out the way,” she said as she poured some of the water over the tooth and she lifted the prize, washed it in the rest of the water and handed it to Terry.

“Thanks, Mrs Hayes,” Terry said as he placed the soapy tooth in its slot. He grimaced and nearly shot it out again.

“Rinse it under cold water,” Hazer said.

“Didn’t think of that.”

So Terry had retrieved his tooth. They made it to the registry office on time and him and Katie were as happy as any young couple on this planet.

The Irish trouble

The night had gone well. It was Austin's birthday. The gang had visited the Ship, George and Dragon, Red Lion and ended the night in the Swan. Austin, of course, was pissed as a fart after the boys had supplied him with copious amounts of beer and spirits, and he could, by the way, drink enough to sink a battleship, but by closing time he couldn't stand.

"What we doing now?" Teddy asked. "Has the landlord [Cecil Marsh] called last orders?"

"Up our house. I'll expect Jock will have a carry out," Hazer shouted over the noisy pub clientele.

So Plummy, Raff, Teddy and Hazer helped Austin onto his feet, each one taking turns assisting him on the uphill walk to Jock's house. As they turned up into Sevenoaks Road, Austin had to be carried so Hazer grabbed his head and shoulders and Raff had his feet. Plummy and Teddy were walking ahead about halfway up the hill that is Sevenoaks Road. A car stopped, facing the boys. Hazer was a bit puzzled when five blokes got out of the car and headed towards them.

Teddy must have known something because he took off like a frightened rabbit, pursued by one of these fellows.

Raff turned to Hazer. "Looks like trouble."

Hazer nodded, but realised he had Austin's head in his hands. The first bloke went to throw a punch at Hazer, who ducked and dropped Austin. Austin's head bounced off the pavement. The noise of 'argh!' left his mouth. Raff was quickly into action. The first assailant was caught with a perfect right cross. He crumpled to the ground as if he hit by a steam train.

Raff was on his toes ready for the next assailant. A short

right to the solar plexus doubled him up. Then a knee to his lower jaw nearly took his head off. Down he went, a groan coming from his battered lips. Meanwhile, Hazer had caught his assassin with a couple of clean jabs to the head, then a right to the jaw, making him stagger backwards. The blood started to leave his mouth covering his clean white shirt. Plummy jumped on his back. The job was done. The fourth assassin was left. Raff caught him with a short jab as he turned to run. Hazer grabbed him by the collar and nutted him several times in the face; he sank to the floor, out cold as were his three mates. Then they could hear Teddy. He wasn't a fighter but always seemed to cause fights

"Help help!"

Raff run up the hill, pulled Teddy's nemesis off him, cracked a couple of rights to his mouth and nose whilst holding him up with his left hand, then let him fold to the ground unconscious.

"Fucking hell, what was that about?" Plummy screamed, the adrenaline making him feel like Tarzan.

Hazer shook his head. "Don't know."

Raff was seething. "Bastards."

Plummy was laughing as he picked up a brick from somewhere and proceeded to smash the headlights and front windscreen of the car. Then he wrenched the door open, let the handbrake off, and waved the vehicle goodbye as it lurched side to side on its way down Sevenoaks Road, hitting the fencing before coming to rest along the link road.

Hazer and Raff picked Austin up if as if nothing had happened and made their way up to Jock's for a nightcap. Plummy was dancing besides them, explaining what had just happened to the whole of Wymering. If anyone was awake to hear it, that is

The next morning, Austin had a bump on his head the size

of a cricket ball.

"How did I get this?" he asked Hazer.

"Sorry Mick, I dropped you. Want a cuppa?"

They had awoke on the sofa; the sun coming through a chink in the curtains.

The smell of bacon was coming from the kitchen. Jock was at work burning breakfast.

A week or so later, when Teddy resurfaced, the truth came out. He and a couple of others had picked on one of the paddies in the Clacton, and they were out for revenge. This was Wymering. In those days, the Irish boys were all young bucks, living in a couple of caravans behind Mrs Carr's house in Harleston Road and it took several years before they could integrate with the local lads.

Hazer could hardly remember what had happened, as it was over as most fights were, in a couple of minutes. But Plummy, who had never been in a scrap before, remembered every split second and would repeat the episode to anyone who would listen for several years. Hazer just remembered Plummy dancing up Sevenoaks Road after the incident as if he had won the World Heavyweight Championship, and Austin's groan as his head hit the floor.

Opportunity rocks

The Swan was a pub, a bit like the Wild West. Cecil and Edie were the landlord and landlady. And although the clientele were like the wild bunch, they had the greatest respect for them. So if Cecil said that's enough, everybody accepted it. There was a television programme just out called *Opportunity Knocks*. So it was some bright spark's idea to pretend auditions for said programme were to be held in the public bar of the Swan. The rumour was spread around Cosham so all the eccentric amongst the populous would know the auditions were to be held on a Saturday night at 8 pm sharp.

So the scene was set. Several of the eccentrics had registered, the genuine people – those who could sing and dance – were told the truth except for Freddie Ware, who the boys enjoyed watching anyhow. The table with the judges was placed in front of the makeshift stage.

Jock was the head judge dressed in his fur coat. He looked the part. He was joined by George Thorpe, who was also the compere, and Jimmy Martin, who always looked smart, suited and booted.

The place was packed. The would-be contestants were ushered into the Bottle and Jug to be prepared by Ralphie and Moaler.

The first act was greeted with a rapturous roar. He came through the makeshift curtains with just his underpants on. Ralphie had told him he needed a gimmick so stripped him. George went up to him and asked what he was going to do.

"Ladies and gentlemen," he announced. "This contestant is going to sing."

A 'boo' roared out.

"Wait for it!" George was holding back the best bit. "Wait for it… whilst underwater!" he shouted.

A stunned audience watched as Ralphie and Blocker Butler carried in a dustbin full of water, slopping some on the floor. Cecil shook his head as if to say, watch what you're doing you'll drown him.

The contestant took a bow to the roaring crowd. He started to sing. It sounded like a squirrel with his nuts caught in a pair of pliers. Then he submerged his head and shoulders underwater. The bubbles and a muffled sound could be heard as the pub stood silent, not believing what was happening. He must have been running out of air as he surfaced and made a bow.

"More, more!" was all he heard. So down again into the dustbin he went. The pub was in stitches. This went on another couple of times. When George, the compère called a halt to the singing underwater act.

Jock and his fellow judges consulted, then lifted the bits of cardboard with the scores on. The contestant gave another bow. As he left the public bar to return to the Bottle and Jug, leaving wet footprints across the tiled floor, George stood in front of the pub to announce the next act.

"Put your hands together for Tarzan of the Apes!" he shouted.

Through the curtains came Freddie Saunders. He had a pair of Y-fronts on and a string vest. The pub exploded in laughter. Freddie started to do his strongman act, showing his muscles. He was a big man, but a bully if he could get away with it. George handed him a telephone book announcing, "Ladies and gentlemen, Tarzan will now rip this book in half."

Freddie took the book and proceeded to try and rip the telephone directory into two halves. His face was getting red, the strain was making him sweat from his forehead, but try as he could, the book wouldn't give.

George, after five minutes or so of watching Freddie straining, stepped in.

"That must have been the ten-year version. It's a lot thicker," he bellowed, to the laughter-induced audience.

He whispered to Freddie, "Don't give up."

Then two chairs were placed five feet apart, so Freddie could show his strength. He was to lie with his feet on one chair and his head on the other, George informed the audience. Then one chair would be removed, leaving Tarzan levitating on one chair.

Freddie duly lay with his head and shoulders on one chair and his feet on the other, thinking the chair to be removed was the one with his feet resting on.

"And now the chair will be removed," George announced. Freddie tensed his body. The audience knew what was really going to happen, so started to shout, "Remove the chair, remove the chair, remove the chair."

"Are you ready, Freddie?" George asked.

Freddie nodded his head.

"Remove the chair!" You could hear this chant a street away. The anti-climax was thunderous as George removed the chair which supported Freddie's head.

Thwack! The sound echoed around the silent pub, then riotous laughter broke out, followed by clapping and the shouts of "more!". George asked Freddie if he wanted to do it again, but he declined.

The judges offered the verdict, but George had tried to placate Freddie by re-introducing him as the comedy Tarzan act. The next act was introduced – standing on the head harmonica player who couldn't stand on his head. So he was held up by his feet by Blocker and Johnny Gregory. Then he tried to play. This act didn't go down as well as the others. The pub was getting bored. A bag of damaged tomatoes had been acquired from Gregory's fruit and veg cart. The first hit the floor in front of the harmonica player who was immediately dropped by Blocker and Gregory. Cecil rushed from behind the bar.

"That's it, no more or it's off," he yelled.

So the tomato throwers stopped.

The judges gave the verdict. The crowd clapped, the harmonica player bowed and left through the curtains.

The next act was the juggler who couldn't juggle. He didn't last long, then it was the turn of Cosham's own Bob Dylan. His name was Jeffrey, but most of his life was spent under the influence of narcotics – not cannabis, but the hard stuff. He had his own guitar and did manage to put a few chords together and would try to match his words to the chords in somewhat of a chaotic way.

George hushed the crowd. "Ladies and gentlemen, silence please. Our next act is one of our very own." He paused, letting his audience feel the tension. "Let me introduce you to…" Another pause. "Cosham's answer to Mr Bob Dylan."

"Jeffrey!" the pub roared. "Jeffrey, Jeffrey Jeffrey!"

Jeff was waiting behind the curtains. He was sucking up the praise before making his grand entrance.

"Everyone has got to have a gimmick. Jeff," Moaler and Ralphie had informed him as the silver paint started to harden on Jeffrey's naked body. "Take your underpants off." Jeff was so out of it he obeyed them.

The curtains opened. Jeffrey stood there like a silver statue, his guitar covering his naughty bits. They had even painted his guitar. Jeff started to strum and sing some folkish sort of songs. But the audience was laughing so loud nobody could hear him. After a few numbers, George had to step in, "Thank you, thank you," as he pushed Jeff back through the curtains.

Cecil had told George that was enough. So George brought the evening's Swans Palladium night to a close. The aftermath was Jeffrey had to go to hospital as Ralphie and Moaler had painted him in silver lead paint. He nearly croaked it. The paint was courtesy of Portsmouth City Council, where Mr Ralph was employed. Jeffrey recovered and was seen around Cosham singing with his guitar for a couple of years until the drugs got the better of him.

The funfair, Southsea

Hillside was still the choice during the weekdays with the boys all trying to pull a bird to get their end away. Hazer and his mates were getting a reputation for only going with girls for what they could get, which was true. They would date a girl for a few weeks – not weekends as that was drinking time – get their wicked way, then ditch her, so the girls of Hillside were reluctant to date Hazer and his mates.

So it was to Southsea and the funfair on some occasions to try and pull a young lady that they would travel. The girls would all be hanging around the waltzer, a very fast ride, all trying to look like the latest film starlet, giggling if a young lad smiled or whistled at them. The boys knew that most of them would be thumbing a lift home to Leigh Park as the buses would finish running before the funfair shut. It must be said that some of the girls were a bit loose with their morals.

One night, Hazer and Teddy decided to visit the fair. They arrived at about 9:30, went to the hot dog stand for a standard hot dog, swallowing a Coca-Cola to wash it down.

"Hello, gorgeous," Teddy said to a rather plain-looking girl who blushed at his comments.

Hazer looked over Teddy's shoulder to see who he was talking to. She smiled as Hazer introduced himself, interrupting Teddy's chat-up lines.

"Where are you from?" Hazer asked.

"Leigh Park," she answered.

Teddy winked at Hazer.

"Where in Leigh Park?" Hazer inquired.

"Up by the Rover," she answered, getting a bit bolder.

"I know that area quite well," Hazer continued.

Teddy was getting left out of the conversation so started to try and change the tack.

"You got any mates?" he interrupted.

She ignored the question and continued to talk to Hazer.

"So how you getting home?" Hazer was feeling lucky.

"With my mates on the last bus," she answered.

Teddy butted in again. "Where's your mates?"

She shook her head and pointed to the bumper cars, then turned to continue talking to Hazer.

"What you doing down here?" It was her turn to ask questions.

"Just hanging around," Hazer answered. "Bit boring, really."

"Yeah, is a bit but my mates like it here," she replied.

"Do you fancy a hot dog?" Hazer inquired.

She shrugged his shoulders. "Yeah, alright."

Teddy was left in the cold.

"What's your name?" she asked.

"John, what's yours?"

"Miss F," she replied.

"This is corny, but do you come here often?"

"No. It's my first time," she answered.

"What about your mates?" Teddy interrupted.

She turned to Teddy. "Some of them come here quite a lot."

Hazer's mind was in chat-up mode, so he got in before Teddy could reply to the young lady.

"Where do you work?" he asked as innocently as he could.

"Twilfit," came her answer. "Where do you work?"

Hazer thought for a minute. Would he tell her a load of bullshit, i.e. he was an actor or in a pop group, or the truth?

"On the buildings," came out of his mouth.

"My dad works on the buildings. He's a bricky."

"What do you do?" She seemed genuinely interested.

"Digging holes mostly," Hazer shrugged, thinking he had blown it.

"I bet that's hard work."

"Yeah, is a bit."

Teddy was getting left out and was becoming a bit anxious.

"You must have a mate for me," he blurted out.

The young girl turned and pointed to a rather large girl coming off the waltzer.

"Her name's Miss J."

Teddy looked at Hazer with gritted teeth. Hazer tried not to smile but couldn't help himself.

"She looks nice, Ted," he said, his face beaming.

"You…" Teddy was about to call Hazer a wanker but stopped in mid-sentence.

The large young girl seemed to skip through the air as she joined them.

"This is Teddy and I'm John Hayes." Hazer introduced himself and Teddy with a confident smile.

"This is my mate. Miss J," Miss F said as she linked arms with her friend. "John's going to buy us a hot dog."

Hazer looked at Teddy, who grinned, thinking, "Got you back Hazer. Two hot dogs, that's two and sixpence."

"Two hot dogs please," Hazer reluctantly asked the stallholder.

"Want onions?" came his gruff reply.

Hazer looked at the girls who both nodded.

"Brown or red?" came the next question.

The girls both said 'Red" at the same time.

Hazer turned to the stallholder.

"I heard," he said.

Hazer thought, "He's a happy bunny, definitely in the

wrong job." He handed the hot dogs down to the girls, holding his hand out for payment at Hazer, who placed the coins in his palm.

"Thank you," Hazer said, receiving a nod on reply.

"John's going to give us a lift home," Miss F informed her friend who gave Hazer a big smile before going into a deep conversation with her friend, Miss F.

"What's she saying?" Teddy was trying to earwig.

Hazer shrugged his shoulders. "Dunno."

"Where's your car?"

"In the car park at the back."

So the foursome made their way to Hazer's dad's car. The girls followed behind, still with their arms linked.

"That's a nice car, John," Miss F said.

Teddy butted in. "It's his dad's."

"Yeah, but he lets me use it all the time," Hazer retorted. Teddy was trying to get his own back.

Johnny unlocked the car, got in, leaned across, and opened the passenger door. No central locking or seat belts in those days.

"Jump in." He indicated to his new slender friend, patting the front seat as he did. "Teddy and your mate can get in the back," he added.

The young lady joined Hazer on the front seat. The other two squeezed into the rear seats. Hazer started the engine, turned on the lights, checked the mirror (not to see what was behind but to make sure his hair was still in place). It was the copious amounts of Brylcreem that made it stiff as a board, it would take a gale force winds to move it out of place. Teddy was silent in the back, as the car moved off through the dark, moonless night.

Hazer was concentrating on the road, the front seat passenger was as silent as a lamb as they travelled past

Commercial Road, Twyford Ave on to Hilsea, the Lido on the left as he crossed the bridge into Cosham.

"What way you going?" the girl beside Hazer asked.

"I thought we would go along the top of the hill. It's nice this time of night, we can see the lights of Pompey, if that's alright with you."

Miss F looked at Hazer, her face lit up by the dashboard. She smiled, "OK, but we can't be that late."

"Don't worry, I'll get you home in time. Promise. Won't we Ted?"

There was just a grunt from the rear seats. Hazer looked in his mirror. Teddy and his partner had disappeared below the seat line.

"You two alright?"

Another grunt came up from the rear seat.

Hazer reached the George on top of Portsdown Hill.

"Shall we stop and see the lights?" he asked.

"Don't mind," Miss F answered quietly.

So Hazer pulled off the Hill Road, his headlights disappearing into the night. Portsmouth in all its glory was on display like a bejewelled island, the lights twinkling on and off as the mood took them.

"Looks great, don't you think?" he asked his front-seat friend. He had used this patter many times before.

She wriggled her bum across the bench seat till she was touching Hazer.

"Yeah, looks really nice," she whispered.

Then the noise from the back interrupted the silence.

"Where is it?"

"Not there. Down a bit."

"Agh! Not there. Up a bit."

"Fuck me." Teddy's head appeared over the seat. "Turn the light on. I can't find her fanny." With that, a hand dragged him back down.

"It's here."

"Where?"

"That's it. Yes, you're near!"

"Fuck. Turn the light on."

"Wait, I got it."

"That's it, you alright?"

A groan and rocking movements engulfed the car. The girl next to Hazer laughed. Hazer joined her.

"My mate's really terrible."

Then a loud scream vibrated around the inside of the car. Teddy's head popped up again. His face was running with sweat. He smiled. "You two alright?"

Hazer shook his head. "I think we had better get these two home."

He took the girl out once more but no luck.

Not being in love

"Hazer. What you up to?" Ernie Littlefield asked as Hazer left the club next to a young lady with short, cropped ginger hair.

Hazer shrugged. "Come here a minute," Ernie gestured.

"What's up, Ern?"

Ernie was a wise man and he looked after his boys. Hazer had taken this young lady home on several occasions, which was unusual on Hazer's part.

"Come here."

"What's up, Ern?"

"Look, take these. You might need them."

With that, Ern handed Hazer a packet of three. Hazer had never used them or bought them before.

"Ain't got no money, Ern."

"Just take them and be careful."

Hazer took the packet of three from Ernie, trying to hide them from his ginger-haired walk home.

"What's he give you?"

"Nothing, just…" Hazer stopped mid-sentence.

She looked at him with a curious smile on her face. Hazer behaved as casual as he could as she went to put her arm through his. But this wasn't done till you were out of sight of your mate, so he walked on, with her following behind. As soon as they were out of sight of Hillside, Hazer let her catch up.

"Why do you do that?"

"Do what?"

"You know, ignore me?" she complained

"I don't know. It's just…" Hazer never had an answer. His

shit bravado was all that mattered.

The walk home to the Isle of Wight estate, took you past the church. Wymering Church – 800 years old, the graveyards where Hazer and his mates had invoked the devil to join them when they were 13 years old – was on the left as they walked down Wymering Lane.

"This is not the way home," she complained.

"I thought we would go along the alley." This runs alongside the railway lines. Still does.

"There might be rats," she said.

"I'll protect you." Hazer was now a knight in the shiniest armour since armour was invented, i.e. 13th century. The walk ended with a kiss, cuddle and you can visualise the rest. His knees were killing him for days, but he never forgot the smell of lacquer for the rest of his days.

The Kontiki incident

"I'll go knap," Rolphy said.

Obviously he had a brammer (a good hand). The boys were playing the brilliant game of knap. It was a Sunday dinner hour in the Clacton, Freddy Ware was up at the bar entertaining everybody. The pub was like hundreds of other pubs throughout the country.

"Fuck me, Ron not again," Austin said. Ronnie had the last two hands and was at least 30 bob up. "Alright, let's see what you got." Rolphy started to lay his hand, ace of spades. The lads laid their lowest spades, king of spades. The lads laid their next lowest card, then the pub went silent, the door swung open like a John Wayne movie. In came a team of gruff-looking monsters, six of them looking around the Clacton like they owned it. "Fucking hell, look at them." Teddy seemed to shrink in his seat.

Rolphy looked up from his kitty-winning hand and commented, "Fuck me Hazer, you keep fighting like you do. You'll end up like him," pointing to a rather large gentleman some six feet nine inches tall who looked like a steam train had hit him doing 100 mph.

Hazer shuffled in his seat. "Ron, looks like this could go off."

"What you mean?"

"I think they're looking for me."

Cummo said, "Hang on, wait a minute," then left.

"What the fuck do they want you for?"

It was a long, long, long, long story, but it was a glorious night. Hazer. Erky and Ray Bushell had had a load of beer so decided, in their infinite wisdom, to visit the Kontiki Bar nightclub on Hayling Island. They left the pub in high spirits, journeyed over the bridge to Hayling, driving as normal as anyone could being over the limit along the front. Some idiot overtook them at speed, which was not in the law allowed. Also, they cut Hazer up, clipping the side of Jock's new motor, damaging the wing. Hazer, with his brain not functioning, pursued the vehicle to the Kontiki car park. The headlights of the soon-to-be gladiators glared at each other. "Fuck me Hazer, what the fuck you doing?" Ray wasn't a fighter but he had the bollocks to go off the top board in the Lido for a laugh.

It was like the OK Corral. The lights of both vehicles were still on as the five from Leigh Park stood waiting to accept the surrender of the three. Jock had always taught Hazer to be sly in battle, and get the first one in.

So Erky, Hazer and Ray Bushell stood against one giant and four rather large gentlemen.

"Just give me your name and insurance company and I'll sort it out tomorrow," Hazer pleaded.

"Fuck off, midget," came the reply.

"Look, we don't want trouble," but Erky was interrupted.

"You want to fucking try it, mush?"

"Look mate," Erky entreated the enemy.

"Don't fucking make me, you fucking wanker."

Well, Jock always had half a pickaxe handle under the seat of his car. And Hazer had concealed this weapon upon his body, i.e. in his Crombie overcoat.

"Look, we don't want trouble. Let's shake on it," Hazer said as he held his left hand out.

The opposition didn't know what to think as Hazer approached them. Jock said be devious. They weren't on their guard as Hazer produced the pickaxe handle, first striking the one on his left across his face. The next blow hit his mate on the chin. Erky had collared one of the others, then it was the giant's turn, David versus Goliath. But he wasn't Goliath. The first blow caught him full in the face. He sank to his knees. Hazer just kept hitting him. Erky dragged him off. "You'll kill him!" he shouted.

Because he was so tall, Hazer thought he was still up for it, but he was on his knees and still as tall as Hazer.

The bouncers ran out of the club. "What's going on here?"

"They fell over. I think they must be pissed," Ray Bushell said. It was his only contribution.

"It's closing time soon," Rolphy said.

"What you going to do?"

Hazer shrugged. "Don't know."

There were no pool tables, no cues to use as weapons. It was just guts. They were waiting for the bell to ring for last orders. Rolphy, Trevor Davis, said, "We are here but Corrigan was too pissed to know what was going on." Then Cummings came back.

"Alright, John?" Cummings always called Hazer 'John' in a really posh voice.

"Yeah, suppose so."

His hand went inside his jacket and brought out a Smith and Western starting pistol. Johnny was in the Merchant Navy and had access to all sorts of weapons. Hazer, whose heart was beating louder than any drum The Beatles ever played, approached his would-be assailants.

This was fucking hard, but Hazer had to do it.

"You waiting for me?"

"What makes you think that?"

"Well you don't come 'ere often, do you?"

Then Sonner Jones interrupted.

"You do this?"

"Don't know."

"He reckons you did."

"Don't know."

"Any of you come after me."

"What, you tosser," one of Sonner's entourage said.

"Look, Sonner. They started it, not me." Hazer pleaded. Hazer had known Sonner from his days living in Wymering and knocking around with Boomer.

Sonners shrugged his shoulders as Hazer added, "They would have beat the shit out of us."

With that, Hazer opened his jacket to reveal the pistol, which was really a starting gun. Sonner blew out his cheeks.

There were five of them, and only Hazer and Erky who Sonner also knew. "Well," Hazer said as he stood back, away from his would-be assailants. He was well out of range, if he was set upon.

Sonner looked at Hazer and knew if this happened, the repercussions would have been never ending.

"Alright, calm down," Sonner said.

"I'm calm."

"Come on, you lot, let's drink up."

With that, the boys from Leigh Park downed their beers and left. Hazer re-joined his mates, his hands still shaking. He has never forgotten that night and to this day regrets what he did to Gabbie.

Falling in love

It was just a normal night over at Hillside when Hazer spotted a rosy-cheeked, round-faced, turned-up nosed, blue-eyed girl wearing a woollen bomber hat. She was among several of her mates who Hazer previously had walked home, trying to play table tennis. Her smile seemed to cross the room as a lighthouse's beam crosses the sea.

"Who's that Hazer?" asked Teddy. "Haven't seen her before."

"I know you haven't been over here for a while," Teddy answered. Hazer had been working late and then straight in the pub with Jock and the gang

"I might get to know her," Hazer winked.

"She don't like you," Teddy answered.

"How do you know?"

"She told me she reckons you only go out with girls for what you can get."

Which was in fact the truth, but most young men only went out with girls for what they could get. So the young lady was telling the truth as Hazer had gone out with a couple of her acquaintances, she must have heard first hand.

Hazer couldn't take his eyes off her as she tried to hit the table tennis ball across the net, failing miserably most of the time. Hazer went to the toilet to check his hair was still in place as most young men did. His Tony Curtis haircut was a bit floppy, so he combed it back into place, ready to try his luck with the young maiden. He came out of the toilet to find Teddy, his arms around her, teaching her how to hold the paddle.

"You wanker," he whispered in Teddy's ear.

Teddy turned and smiled.

"This is Jenny," he smirked. "She's my new girlfriend.'

Hazer could have strangled him.

"Nice to meet you, Jenny," he said, all the time thinking about strangling Teddy.

"Why don't you like me?" Hazer asked.

Jenny was turning bright red at such a direct question.

Teddy saved the day. "It's because you let one of her best mates down."

"Which one?"

Teddy laughed. "All of them."

Hazer turned away, not saying anything and joined the footballers out the back on the five-a-side or as many a-side as they could get on the pitch.

It was just before Christmas when Raff got married to Joannie after a rapid courtship. They moved into a small flat in North End.

So Hazer lost one of his best drinking buddies to marriage, still working alongside Boomer and the gang going to Hillside, whenever he could. He just couldn't get this girl out of his head. But she still wouldn't speak to him, even though Teddy had given up on her or she had given him the push.

So Hazer tried to make her jealous by going out with one of her best mates. This still didn't work. Hazer was falling hook, line and sinker. He couldn't get her out of his head.

Lying in bed one night, a tear tumbled down his cheek. He hadn't cried in a very long time. Not since he was 16 and his ma (grandmother in Scotland) died. Jock had received a telegram from his sister Esther, telling him his mother was on death's door. So Jock and Hazer had driven to Glasgow through the night in Jock's Vauxhall Krista, arriving at Bob's in the early morning. As soon as it was possible, they visited Jock's mum in Glasgow Infirmary, Jock had always tried to keep in touch, but with no telephones, it was by mail. Aud wrote her a letter every week with the news of her grandchildren on the south coast.

The funeral was a quiet affair with just family present. Then it was to the Clearand bars for the wake. Hazer had a couple of pints, then Dinky asked if he fancied going over the Barrowland, and so the boys left the older members and joined Dinky's mates to visit the night clubs and bars, but they were refused entry to one club because the bouncer accused Hazer of causing trouble the previous week to which Hazer replied, "Wasn't here last week, I'm English." The bouncer's reply was, "Fuck off you wee Sassenach."

As Hazer said, goodnight to Dinky, his thoughts were of his mother and as Dennis boarded the bus for Castlemilk, he turned and walked over the bridge. The Clyde rolled under him cold and grey, slowly reaching for the comfort of the Irish Sea. Hazer stood looking over the parapet as the streetlights danced on this forbidding mass below him. His brain was working overtime. He remembered the newspaper cutting of his uncle Bob getting arrested naked after swimming the Glasgow edifice. He had a bet of five shillings with somebody that he could not swim this imposing river. He had stripped off naked and swam the Clyde. On going back to collect his winnings, the people he had the wager with had stolen his clothes, and the few coppers he had in his pocket. So there he was, drunk, freezing cold in the middle of Glasgow, naked as the day he was born. The tram they were running in Glasgow in the '50s came along and Bob gave the female conductress the shock of her life as he jumped on the back. The police were called and he made the *Glasgow Herald* headlines. The tears started coming as his thoughts turned to his ma, this little old lady who sat with him when he was a boy every summer for two weeks of his and Jock's visit.

Raff was settled in his flat so decided to have a flat-warming party. Hazer had found another bird in the George and Dragon. After a while of chatting her up and buying her numerous Babychams, she agreed to accompany him to Raff and Joan's party.

Hazer knocked on the door. The music could be heard in the street.

"Come in, mate," Raff beckoned.

The party was in full flow as Hazer and his companion entered.

"Want a beer?" KB asked.

"Yeah. Brown ale be nice."

"What about…?" KB looked at the young lady.

"What you want?" Hazer asked her.

"Babycham, if you got it."

KB turned to the table, which was full of bottles, glasses and nibbles, and brought back a brown ale and a Babycham in a tall glass.

"Cheers, Ken!" Hazer thanked Kenny then looked around the room. There sat on the sofa next to Teddy was the love of his life.

Hazer went over, leaving his lady friend talking to Kenny.

"Alright, Ted. Thought you two had split." Hazer was jealous as fuck.

Teddy was a bit uncomfortable as he wriggled in his seat.

"Hello Jenny," Hazer smiled, hoping for a smile in return.

"Who's that?" Teddy asked pointing to Hazer's escort. Hazer thought for a moment, then realised he couldn't remember her name. He shrugged his shoulders. "I picked her up in the George."

The night went on, Hazer got steadily drunk, as did most of the blokes. When he awoke, everyone was gone. He let himself out as quietly as he could and drove home in the early hours, tears streaming down his cheeks. As a few touched his lips, it tasted of salt.

A few days later, the Clacton was full. It was the Saturday before Christmas and the local football had been called off because of the bad weather. Ernie Bradwell was munching a steak and kidney pie. When a bit fell out and landed on the table, he automatically flipped it in the direction of Lenny H. It landed on his new white shirt. Lenny H left his seat and went to the bar, bought a steak and kidney pie, opened the crust and poured the contents on Ernie's head. The laughter rang out. Ernie, not to be outdone, splashed some of his drink over Corrigan. Corrigan splashed some of his drink on Frankie M. Then it erupted, a full-grown beer fight. The whole gang were laughing as they drenched each other with beer and steak and kidney pies. The floor was like someone had been sick a hundred times. Bits of pie were floating in brown splits and best bitter.

"You lot had better clean this up." Bert the landlord was handing a couple of buckets and mops to Lenny. H and Hazer as the boys were still laughing as they took it in turns to get the Clacton back to normality. This was when Raff spotted a face pressed against the window. He looked again. It was gone.

"I swear I saw Jenny's face in the window," Raff told Hazer as he knew Hazer fancied her wicked. Many years later, Jenny told me the story. She was on Kathy Parkins' shoulders, looking through the window – which was above head height by the way – to see who was in the pub when Raff spotted her face pressed against the windowpane. When she saw Raff point to her, she screamed and wet herself, drowning Kathy.

"You sure it was her?" Hazer asked.

"Yeah, think so."

Hazer was as puzzled as Raff.

So on the Monday he saw Jenny, or bombhead, as he had nicknamed her, playing table tennis again. So he took his chance. As the ball rolled towards him, he picked it up as Jenny came to retrieve it. He gave her his biggest smile as he handed her back the ball and she actually smiled back.

"Fancy a game with me later?" He couldn't believe it when she blushed and said, "Alright."

Hazer's reply of "Great" was drowned out by the music. So table tennis it was. Jenny was not a match for Hazer, but he tried to go as easy as he could, letting her win a few points. After they finished, Hazer took the bat off Jenny and for the first time touched her hand. He felt as if he had reached the summit of Mount Everest.

"Do you fancy a coffee?" he murmured.

Her face turned a shade of red, not knowing after all this time, whether to accept Hazer's offer.

"Please," Hazer entreated.

Jenny, after a long pause, said, "Only a coffee, John." She called him John.

Hazer seemed to float on his bumper boots as he escorted Jenny down the steps to the coffee bar.

"Two coffees, Peg." Peggy smiled as she knew Hazer had a crush on his pretty young maiden.

"Do you want sugar?" he asked Jenny.

"Two, please," she shyly replied. So Hazer carefully placed two sugar lumps into the coffee cup. Then after placing three in his, he carried the cups to a corner table. They sat down. Hazer couldn't take his eyes off her. All the patter he had used on so many other girls just would not come out of his mouth. They sat there in complete silence. Hazer drank his coffee down trying not to slurp. Jenny took little sips.

"Do you fancy another game later?" He couldn't think

of anything else to say. She looked at him and smiled before answering. "OK."

So after another game, Jenny re-joined her mates, who were practising the jive, skirts twirling as they spun each other around.

Hazer walked home that night on his own; his thoughts were all over the place, wondering if Jenny liked him after all. The next night at Hillside, Hazer approached Jenny.

"Do you fancy a coffee later?"

Jenny nodded, blushing as she said, "Yes, OK."

So it was coffee, table tennis, but that was all. Hazer hadn't asked to walk her home, but Jenny was actually talking to him and smiling.

It was the Friday dance night at Hillside, but because Hazer was one of the boys who couldn't dance, he was a wallflower. All the girls danced with each other, a few boys joining in, taking two girls as they bopped to the music of Dave Dee and the Bostons', later Dave Dee, Dozy, Beaky, Mick and Tich. Hazer had drunk a few pints of brown split in the Clacton. There was a slope outside the Clacton and it was custom to have a piss race down the slope. So the boys stood on the top with their willies hanging out, seeing whose pee would go the furthest.

So over Hillside, Ernie was at the door collecting the half-crown entrance fee.

"You lot, behave yourselves," Ernie said as he threw the half-crowns into a cashbox.

"Yes, Ern, you know us," Plummy laughed.

"Yes, I know you," Ernie said as he playfully clipped Plummy behind the ear hole.

The hall was dark, the band playing so loud you had a job to hear anyone or be heard unless you shouted.

Jenny and her mates were in deep conversation as Hazer,

accidentally on purpose bumped into her.

"Sorry!" he shouted above the band who were playing a Gene Vincent classic, 'Be-Bop-a-Lula'.

Jenny turned and smiled.

"You been up the Clacton?" she asked. Hazer could only lipread what she said.

"Yeah, had a couple of pints. That's all."

Jenny laughed at Hazer's explanation, telling her he wasn't drunk before she had asked.

Hazer was trying to get the bottle up to ask if he could walk her home. They both stood looking at each other. The band stopped playing. Hazer leant over and whispered in Jenny's ear.

"What, I couldn't hear you?" she mouthed as the band started up again.

Hazer bucked up the courage, hoping that he wouldn't get a rejection.

"Can I walk you home?" came out of his mouth.

Jenny looked at him. Hazer was longing for the answer to be yes.

Jenny blushed as she nodded.

"Does that mean yes?" Hazer's heart was beating.

Jenny nodded again.

"What time do you have to be in?" Most girls, even though over 16, had to be in by a proper time. Jenny was no different.

Jenny muttered, "Nine thirty."

The club didn't close till 10 o'clock, but Hazer didn't care, he was walking Jenny home.

The hands on the clock behind the serving hatch seemed to take forever to reach 9 o'clock. He kept looking over at Jenny, hoping she wouldn't change her mind.

"You alright, Hazer?" Ernie asked.

"Yeah, Ern, I'm great."

"Do you need any?" Ern asked, meaning a packet of three.

"No thanks, Ern," Hazer's reply brought a smile to Ernie's face. "Perhaps this is the one," he thought to himself. Hazer was waiting by the door as Jenny gathered her coat from the hooks outside the ladies toilet. She joined him at the door, putting her coat on against the winters cold air.

Hazer turned and waved to his mates as he ushered Jenny out through the double doors of Hillside youth club. Jenny was really shy, so Hazer had to make the most of the conversation, telling her all about himself, trying to prove he was a nice guy, not the one who only went with girls for what he could get.

They reached the alley at the top of Sixth Avenue that led to Fifth Avenue where Jenny lived.

Jenny stopped. "I'll have to go. My dad will be walking the dog," she uttered.

"That's OK," Hazer said as he went to give her a kiss. But Jenny moved her head so Hazer's smacker hit her on the cheek. Just then, Hazer felt a presence behind him. He turned to see a broad-shouldered bloke with a large nose, square chin and ears drooping like a bloodhound.

"Hello Dad," Jenny called out as the dog accompanying this shadow jumped up at her.

"It's late," Jenny's dad (his name was Len) said in a deep, gruff voice, obviously, put on to frighten any of Jenny's suitors away.

"Won't be long, Dad," Jenny answered, and she gave a big smile. "See you tomorrow," she mouthed to Hazer.

Hazer's heart seemed to leap out of his chest as he let the words sink in.

"Alright," he mouthed back.

That night Hazer seemed to float up Sevenoaks Road. He entered his front room.

"You're home early," his mum enquired. "Is something wrong?"

"No mum. I'm OK, just a bit tired, that's all."

He slept that night as if all his dreams had come true. He was truly in love.

The pylons

Johnny had been courting Jenny for two months. One of his best mates, Micky Austin, was courting, Jenny's mate, Linda. Hazer had left Jock to make his fortune alongside Mick erecting pylons. This was dangerous work, but really well paid. It was alright when they were working local, just on the ground supplying the gangs who erected these metal giants but to get into the real money you had to be in an erection gang. So they signed up to join the other side, which meant they would have to leave home and live in digs, in Weymouth, some 60 miles from Pompey, but in those days with no proper roads it was like 200 miles. They packed their meagre belongings into a couple of rucksacks and caught the train from Cosham station.

"What you think, Mick?" Hazer asked as they booked into a bed and breakfast in the middle of Weymouth. The streets were deserted. It was the beginning of April and the holidaymakers wouldn't arrive till June.

"Dunno," he replied.

Hazer hadn't been away from home since his incarceration at Glen House, so he was a little apprehensive to say the least.

"Sign here," the rather rotund landlady said as she pointed to the bottom of a set of rules. "Your in room 3," she said, as she handed a set of keys to Austin.

"Breakfast starts at 6, dinner at 6 sharp. I'll expect you to be clean at dinner," she added, "No overalls."

Micky and Hazer ascended the stairs to their room and unlocked the door. A double bed confronted them with sheets and pillows. This was luxury. A small sink was on the wall with a mirror above it. A wardrobe was in the corner, open with hangers. Hazer turned to Micky and nodded. This was like a five-star hotel to them.

They threw their rucksacks on the bed and returned down the stairs to explore the town. As they were about to leave, a lean, tall, somewhat well-spoken gentleman introduced himself.

"Hi, I'm Simon." His voice was very posh to Hazer and Micky's ear. They didn't know what to say.

"You here on holiday?" he asked.

"No, working on the pylons," Micky replied.

"Oh my god!" Simon announced.

"What's up?"

"Well, it's not a job I would like."

"What you do, then?"

"I'm in between jobs." Simon seemed embarrassed.

"Would you like to join me? I know all the good pubs."

Hazer looked to Austin and laughed.

"Yeah, alright mate," he said. "We ain't arse bandits."

Simon laughed as he straightened his tie. So the two young lads were escorted by Simon to all the best pubs in Weymouth and Simon behaved like a true gentleman or woman.

The breakfast was looking at Hazer like something from hell. It had to be devoured or he would pay later when he was starving. The fried bread was still dripping as he cut it into pieces, dipping it in the egg yolk.

"You boys in our gang?" a rather short man said to the boys as he sat on their table.

"I'm Jack," he said as he sat down.

Then another three blokes entered, Jack introduced them to Hazer and Austin.

"The lorry be here at 7, so make sure you're ready."

"Yeah, alright," Austin said as he sucked the last dregs out of his teacup.

The lorry drove up outside the digs at exactly 7 o'clock. Micky and Hazer joined the rest of the gang on the back of the lorry sitting down to keep the wind off.

They arrived at the site. This great giant of the structure was looking down on them. Hazer and Micky looked up at it. It seemed to disappear into the stratosphere.

"Wake up you two!" It was Jack.

Then the questions started.

"You scared of heights?"

"You got anything wrong with you?"

And on and on and on. Hazer and Micky must have answered all the questions right because they were handed a belt with two podgers in the podger holders. A podger is a large spanner at one end and a pointed bit at the other.

"OK, have you ever been up a pylon?" Jack was really strict.

Hazer had to open his mouth.

"Yeah, there was a sparrowhawk nesting in one of the arms and I got its eggs."

Jack laughed. "Egging was you?" Obviously he had done the same as a boy.

"OK. You two up, you go to the top arms, go right to the end and I'll tell you when to come down."

Hazer and Micky started to climb. No safety harness in those days.

(If you look at the pylon, there are small bolts sticking out on each leg. This is what you climbed to the top with, no other aides.)

"You alright Mick?" Hazer asked as he looked across to Micky who was clinging to the opposite leg of the pylon.

Micky nodded, but Hazer could see he wasn't a happy person.

"Come on Mick. Race you to the top."

Hazer never had a fear of heights. He had been climbing trees since his childhood.

But Micky was a bit apprehensive

"Look at that view." Hazer was pointing at the countryside of Dorset. Micky was clutching onto the steel. His fingertips seemed to make imprints in the pylon.

"You two alright?" Hazer gave a startled look as Jack had joined them. He was like a monkey as he joined the two beginners.

"You'll get used to it," he said as he gave the boys the lowdown.

"What we do is check each bolt. Make sure it's done up tight and replace any that's not right. If the erection gang has left any bolts out, we put them in and make sure they're done up, OK lads?" Jack was smiling as he stood up balancing on a piece of steel, four inches wide, some 100 feet off the ground.

"Stay up here for an hour, then come down to the lower arms, OK?"

Hazer and Austin nodded.

After an hour looking over the Dorset countryside, Jack whistled and the two training monkeys climbed down to the lower level.

"Right, start checking the bolts. Make sure you don't miss any," Jack said as he grinned.

By the time the lorry came to pick them up, Hazer and Austin were knackered, climbing up and down all day.

So it was day in, day out but Hazer and Micky would write home (no telephones) twice a week to Jenny and Linda their girlfriends as they told the rest of the gang.

After four weeks, it was time to go home on a long weekend. It seemed to take ages for the steam train to reach Pompey and home. Hazer couldn't wait to see Jenny. His mind was full of worry that she had found somebody else. He and Micky got a taxi, never heard of in those days, home from Cosham station.

Hazer walked through the door. It was 6 o'clock on a Friday. He was expecting a welcome like a long-lost son, but all he got was Jeannie grinning.

"Where's mum?" he asked.

"Over Nan's."

So Hazer dumped his haversack and went over the green to his nan's house.

"Hello, son." His mum said ready to cuddle her baby boy, but Hazer dodged her.

"You alright, Nan? Hazer. Looking around to his mum waiting for her to explain what was going on.

Granddad's been taken ill.

Hazer sat down on the threadbare sofa. "What's up with him?"

His nan answered in a low sort of silent whisper. "He will be alright, I promise." As Hazer sank into her arms, his mind went back to his younger years and his granddad teaching him to do all the things that life would challenge him with.

It was a Friday night. Hazer and Austin had cash in their pockets. The world was theirs.

"Mum, Jeannie's still in the bath!"

"She won't be long."

"Mum! She's been in there an hour!"

"I'll call her."

"Jean, Johnny's waiting to have a bath!"

"He can wait," came the reply.

"Come on Mum, tell her!" Hazer added, "It's getting late, I'll be late!"

"What will you be late for?"

Hazer was really frustrated. He didn't want to tell his mum

he had a date with Jenny.

"Jean, hurry up!" she shouted through the door.

"Coming!" she sang out, knowing anything she could do to annoy her older brother was a victory.

As she left the bathroom, Hazer was waiting outside.

"Thanks sis. Did you clean the bath round?"

Jeannie looked at Hazer. Daggers seemed to enter her soul. "Course I did," came her answer.

"Sorry Jean," Hazer offered up his apology as she disappeared up the stairs to her bedroom.

Jeannie was dating a boy called Mickey Cox. He was a lump of a lad, 6-foot tall, bushy hair, square chin ears a bit large but his only set back was one eye. Hazer had known him from senior school. Mickey hadn't been a sportsman, but he was known to be a tough cookie. He lost his eye playing Robin Hood. The arrow missed the ball and hit poor Mickey. Anyhow, they were in love. Hazer's little sister and Mickey. It was nice. Jock was a bit wary, but Hazer soothed him down, telling him Mickey was alright, so the romance blossomed and the wedding bells summoned.

Hazer scrubbed up as best he could, put on his best clothes, looked in the mirror to make sure he didn't have any unwanted spots, straightened his slimline tie, made sure his hair was untouchable. Quite literally, it was as hard as a hedgehog's bristles.

The journey to Hillside seemed to vanish. His steps were lighter than Fred Astaire's. His heart was beating to think he had been apart from his… for a month was unbearable, but he was a man and had to get tough.

So it was to the Clacton first. Hazer was flushed, the old boys in the corner by the fire were sat as they always were. Hazer ordered a tray of brown splits (they all drank brown splits) and took them over to the old boys. Boo Boo Willit, a hulk of a man, a nose that had seen all the colours of the rainbow stood up. "Thanks," he said. Jimmy Hayward and a couple of the others lifted their pints. "Cheers, young man."

Hazer felt proud that he could buy these old gentlemen a drink.

Jenny was waiting over Hillside. Hazer had had five pints, so was a bit merry.

"What's it like?"

"What's what like?"

"You know what."

"No, what do I know?"

"Working away."

Hazer shrugged. "It's not…"

"I'm knitting you a cardigan," Jenny interrupted.

Hazer didn't know what to say. Nobody had ever knitted anything in his family before.

"Thanks, Jen." Hazer was a little apprehensive.

"What colour do you like?"

Hazer took a deep breath. "Blue, I suppose."

"What about mauve?" she inquired.

Hazer looked at her. "I love any colour," he heard himself say.

So mauve it was. When this knitted woollen object was presented to Hazer, he was quite shocked. He tried it on and went to put his hands in the pockets, but must have missed so tried it again then realised that this masterpiece of woollen mystery didn't possess pockets. He looked at Jenny, a smile on his face.

"Thanks Jen," he uttered.

Not 'no pockets', which was at the back of his mind.

"Does it fit alright?"

Hazer nodded. "Yeah, perfectly," he lied.

"Do you like the colour?"

"My favourite," he lied. Who likes mauve?

So as he tried this cardigan on that Jenny had worked

so hard on whilst he was away climbing these giant steel monoliths. It seemed the right thing to say.

"When you going back?"

"Monday, I think."

She didn't seem happy with Hazer's reply.

That weekend was like a whirlwind centred around Jenny. He borrowed Jock's car on a Saturday night to take Jenny out over the villages at the back of Portsdown Hill. His plan was to try to get Jenny a bit tipsy and try his luck.

So it was the pubs of Denmead and Cowplain. After a while, Hazer noticed that Jenny would not drink in front of him, but every time he went to the toilet he would come back and her glass would be near empty. He was in the Spotted Cow when he'd literally spotted this so he kept using the toilet. But his plan never worked. Jenny could hold her drink better than him. After five pints he was ready to call it a day. Jenny was still as sober as a judge. The gin and bitter lemon never worked. Years later, Hazer was telling his then wife Jenny about his plan backfiring. And she laughed and revealed her thoughts at the time were that Hazer had a weak bladder as he kept going to the toilet.

Hazer and Austin were at the station in Cosham, waiting for the train to transport them back to Weymouth. It was raining that drizzly rain that gets you wet. Micky was puffing on his third Senior Service since arriving at the platform, the rain dripping off his hair and onto the cigarette dipping out the side of his lip.

"What's up Mick?" Hazer could see Micky wasn't himself. He shrugged his shoulders.

"Don't know."

"You alright mate?"

He shrugged his shoulders again.

Hazer tumbled. Micky wasn't happy up on the giants. The steel, his only companion, the thought of falling, was never out of his mind.

The train could be heard in the distance. The gates that crossed Cosham High Street started to lower, the last car just squeezing through the man in the signal box could be seen spinning the large wheel that controlled the gates.

"You don't want to go."

Micky looked at Hazer. Hazer knew the look.

"Alright Mick."

He shook his head. Hazer picked up his small suitcase that held his world.

"You coming?" he gestured to Micky, whose face lit up, the relief of knowing he wouldn't have to face the giants again, lifted.

"Come on, the Ship will be open in half an hour. You can get the first round." Hazer put his arm around Micky's shoulder as the train arrived. The two young men were on the footbridge that led from platform two to platform one. They stood still as the train to Weymouth passed underneath them.

The Ship doors were ajar, the cleaner was just finishing her task. Cleaning up after Sunday night was always heavy as the pub on the Sunday was always packed to the rafters.

Hazer poked his head around the door of the public bar. Frank Nuttall the landlord was busy polishing the array of glasses and replacing them on the shelves behind him.

"Any chance of a pint, Frank?"

He turned, looked at the clock above the open fire, which was crackling into life. It was ten am another half hour before opening.

"Close the door behind you," he said as he lowered one of the pint glasses under the pump, which he began to pull. The beer cascaded into the glass.

To Be Continued

The next instalment is in my head ready to go